"How do you take the gospel to college-educated secular people who may be suspicious of your motives? Ken Lottis has done it, and his memoir is an eye-opening look at missions in a post-Christian culture. Through a series of choices that seem obvious only in hindsight, Ken and his partners discerned how to effectively reach the kind of people whom many of us would write off as hardened to the gospel."

— KAREN LEE-THORP, coauthor of the
BRINGING THE BIBLE TO LIFE Bible studies

"Ken Lottis's storytelling ability is compelling. So is the relational style of discipling-making he and his colleagues modeled among university students in Brazil. *Will This Rock in Rio?* documents a missional approach to personal evangelism that pastors, youth pastors, and parachurch leaders would do well to replicate."

— REV. GREG ASIMAKOUPOULOS, pastor, Mercer Island Covenant
Church; newspaper columnist; author of *Sunday Rhymes and Reasons*

"This book is a moving account of a contemporary reenactment of the relationship style outreach of Jesus. It demonstrates that building relationships is the effective biblical means to building the kingdom of God cross-culturally. Ken shows how it is (and must be) 'exquisitely simple, portable, and transferable.'"

— REV. BURDETTE PALMBERG, pastor emeritus, the Mercer Island
Covenant Church and the International Church of Lucerne, Switzerland

"Ken Lottis invites his readers to relive his missionary journey into Latin American culture decades ago. This is an insightful and useful book for anyone engaging in cross-cultural ministry today."

— RICH BERRY, The Navigators, African American Network

"A remarkable and exciting account of an ordinary young couple and their three children who left home, compelled by the Savior, to travel to a distant land to make disciples for the kingdom of God. Setting aside all of their preconceived notions, they allowed the Scriptures and the Spirit of God to lead them in unique ways to develop a host of followers of Christ and to equip them to teach others. A must-read for those who would allow God to transform their own lives even as they bring followers into the kingdom."

— BUD LINDSTRAND, former CEO, ODS Companies

"I loved every page of Ken's book. What Ken does for us in this masterful narrative is focus the reader on what should matter most to us: people and the kingdom of God! One senses the value Ken, his family, and the Petersens placed on the people they were sent to work among. These were not projects or objects but rather people to love and invest their very lives in."

— LUCIANO DEL MONTE, pastor, Lakeside Church, Guelph, Ontario;
The Navigators, Canada

"This book is an inspiration and encouragement to all who take seriously Christ's call to make disciples of all nations. Ken Lottis and his wife, Carol, model friendship evangelism to Brazilian students, couples, and families. *Will This Rock in Rio?* tells their story in an engaging and readable style."

— HAROLD MILLER, PhD, professor emeritus, University of Minnesota; provost (retired), Northwestern College, St. Paul, Minnesota

"As I read this book, my eyes frequently welled up with tears of awe and respect for Ken and Carol Lottis, and my heart was responding, 'This is it.' These notes from Ken's diaries and memories confirm that scriptural principles and the model of Jesus' life are timeless. The discoveries these guys made in Brazil are filled with jewels for those of us seeking to help people move forward in their search for a relationship with God."

— NANCY RALPH, lawyer, Toronto, Ontario; former board member, The Navigators, Canada

"I have heard it said that the world is not made up of atoms but of stories. Life is a one-and-only story with lessons, joys, and sorrows. This is not just the story of Ken and Carol Lottis but one of the gospel changing them and gaining Brazilian clothes—distinctly non-American and boldly and frighteningly biblical. Friendship trumped methods. Pure motives trumped manipulation. Time and numbers lost their meaning. What counted was friends getting to know the real Jesus of the Bible. The shedding of their American evangelical clothes changed them as much as it changed their new friends. This book will challenge you to rethink how the gospel moves among your friends."

— JERRY WHITE, PhD, president emeritus, The Navigators; author of *The Joseph Road, Dangers Men Face,* and *Honesty, Morality, and Conscience*

"As I read this warm personal history of the ministry of Ken Lottis and Jim Petersen in Brazil, I was given hope for the future. I trust that the young Lottises and Petersens of this generation will find much in this book to help them as they discover in their ministries how God is building the kingdom today. Though no longer young, I found much to help me!"

— REV. MICHAEL FITZGERALD, pastor, Community Covenant Church, Santa Cruz, California

"Ken Lottis is a tremendous storyteller, and story is the medium Jesus chose for the gospel. Relationally rich, warmly humorous, and vulnerably real, Ken walks you through the timeless challenges of crossing cultural barriers with the unadorned kingdom message of Jesus. Spiritual pioneering, humble dependence, and biblical clarity make this an Acts 29 message for today."

— FRED WEVODAU, DMin, director of U.S. Metro Mission, The Navigators

KEN LOTTIS

With Contributions by Jim Petersen

WILL THIS ROCK IN

RIO?

Finding God in an Urban Culture

To Jane —

Thanks for all your wonderful stories. I hope you enjoy reading some of the adventures that Carol and I lived through, in Brazil.

NAVPRESS

NAVPRESS⬤

NavPress is the publishing ministry of The Navigators, an international Christian organization and leader in personal spiritual development. NavPress is committed to helping people grow spiritually and enjoy lives of meaning and hope through personal and group resources that are biblically rooted, culturally relevant, and highly practical.

For a free catalog go to www.NavPress.com
or call 1.800.366.7788 in the United States or 1.800.839.4769 in Canada.

ISBN: 978-1-60006-393-0

Cover design by Arvid Wallen
Cover imagery by Shutterstock
Author photo by Ron Nickel
Personal photos by Ken Lottis and Monte Unger

Some of the anecdotal illustrations in this book are true to life and are included with the permission of the persons involved. All other illustrations are composites of real situations, and any resemblance to people living or dead is coincidental.

Unless otherwise noted, all Scripture quotations in this publication are taken from the *Holy Bible, New International Version* (NIV). Copyright © 1973, 1978, 1984 by International Bible Society. Used by permission of Zondervan. All rights reserved. Another version used is the King James Version.

Library of Congress Cataloging-in-Publication Data

Lottis, Ken.
  Will this rock in Rio? : finding God in an urban culture / Ken Lottis.
    p. cm.
  Includes bibliographical references.
  ISBN 978-1-60006-393-0
  1. Missions--Brazil--Curitiba. 2. Evangelistic
work--Brazil--Curitiba. 3. Navigators (Religious organization) I.
Title.
  BV2853.B6L68 2010
  266'.023730816209045--dc22
                              2009023466

Printed in the United States of America

1 2 3 4 5 6 7 8 / 14 13 12 11 10

To Carol,

who said yes when I asked her to marry me fifty years ago.
And also said yes to the challenges of moving halfway around
the world, learning a new language, and adapting to a new culture,
doing it all with amazing grace, captivating charm, and
affectionate love.

CONTENTS

PREFACE

THROUGHOUT HISTORY, GOD has seemed to take pleasure in departing from patterns we expect of him. He often does something very different using unlikely people.

For example, that fanatical Pharisee named Saul was knocked off his horse while on a mission to protect the purity of first-century Judaism. He changed his name to Paul, did a theological U-turn, and became the first missionary to take the message of Jesus to the non-Jewish world.

Or that small-town German monk who wrote out some notes from his Bible studies and nailed them to the door of his church. He unwittingly triggered a movement that changed the course of history.

And then there's the story of a young man in Southern California who began meeting one-on-one with sailors serving in the U.S. Navy in the 1930s. By the end of World War II, Dawson Trotman was involved with men who called themselves Navigators on more than a thousand ships and military bases. As I write this, I am one of 4,200 Navigator missionaries of sixty-four different nationalities laboring in 103 countries of the world.

It should come as no surprise that this same pattern is evident throughout the earthly ministry of Jesus. He stunned his disciples when he engaged a Samaritan woman in conversation. He was labeled a glutton and a drunkard by religious leaders because of his association with the "wrong crowd." He trashed the commerce that profited from the temple in Jerusalem.

Then there's that amazing story in Mark's gospel (4:35–5:20) when Jesus, "leaving the crowd behind," crossed the Sea of Galilee to the Gentile side of the lake. After weathering a frightening storm, the disciples must have watched in wonder as their Master encountered and healed a scary but needy individual. After instructing the man to "tell [your family] how much the Lord has done for you," Jesus and his disciples sailed back across the lake.

In a similar fashion, this is a story about some very unlikely people who find themselves involved in an extraordinary adventure. Carol and I were raised in small towns in very conservative religious homes, as were Jim and Marge Petersen. In the mid-1960s the four of us were selected by The Navigators to move to Brazil and begin a ministry among university students. For us "leaving the crowd behind" meant saying good-bye to our evangelical upbringings, our colleagues with The Navigators, our families and friends and going "to the Gentile side of the lake." That's what this book is about.

Thus began an adventure that has shaped our lives and the lives of our children and grandchildren. It gave us fresh insight into the gospel, a broader understanding of Christ's Great Commission and the nature of the church. But most of all it allowed us to be participants in God's redemptive and transforming work in the lives of people in some remarkably unique ways.

It is my hope that in reading this story you will be encouraged in your personal adventure with God, that you will find yourself participating in one of these experiences where ordinary people are involved in his extraordinary work. But let me warn you: Such an experience might involve leaving the familiarity of your crowd and crossing to the other side of the street. It might require moving out of your comfort zone and taking initiatives to make some new friends.

ACKNOWLEDGMENTS

THIS STORY WOULD never have happened nor would this book have been written without Jim Petersen. Our friendship began in Minneapolis at Northwestern College in the fall of 1952. We hung out together and stayed in touch for the next ten years. Then early in 1963 he let me know that my name was on a list of candidates to join his team that would pioneer a Navigator ministry in Brazil. He was on the dock in the port of Santos in November of 1964 to greet us when this story started. Forty years later as we vacationed together with our wives in Santa Fe, New Mexico, the idea for this book was born. Since then we've spent many days together along with hours on Skype connections to review what I was writing. Without his notes, journals, and memories, together with his patient coaching, this story would still be a bunch 1s and 0s on my laptop's hard drive.

If my life and this book could be dusted for fingerprints, the imprints of three men would appear over and over again.

During the first few days of my freshman year at Northwestern College, a note appeared in my mailbox from Ed Reis inviting me to meet with him at his apartment a few blocks off campus. That first meeting began a relationship that has had a powerful influence on my life for more than half a century. Ed continues to pray for me every day.

Another friendship begun that fall has remained intact — with Denny Repko. We were roommates in Dinkytown near the campus of the University of Minnesota during my senior year at Northwestern

College. Two years later, in October of 1958, he traveled across the Midwest arriving with only an hour to spare to be best man in my wedding. Denny is my definition of a lifelong friend.

My relationship with Aldo Berndt transcended nationality, culture, and language to establish a unique bond of friendship, unlike anything I had experienced prior or since. He seemed to have an uncanny ability to understand what was deep in the well of my soul, give it great value, and help me draw it to the surface. His influence in my life and in this story is profound.

In carrying out their roles of leadership in The Navigators, Lorne Sanny, George Sanchez, and Jim Downing signed off on the decision to send us to Brazil. Their subsequent trips to visit us provided guidance and affirmation. This story is punctuated with their wisdom.

I met Jack Combs for the first time in São Paulo's chaotic Congonhas International Airport. His cowboy humor and earthy common sense made him an easy guy to partner with when we worked together in Porto Alegre. Our friendship with Jack and Barbara is in the forever category.

There are others whose presence in Brazil contributed to the story you are about to read. The lives of Sue Gliebe, Dan and Suzanne Greene, Fernando and Ieda Gonzalez, Ray and Sharon Rice, Bo and Judy Young, Doug and Evelyn MacKenzie, Don and Marion Caulkins, Dave and Beatrice Hicks, Tom and Dana Steers, and Blake and Shirlee Soule are all visible in between the lines of what I have written.

There is no way that I can convey the value and significance of our many friends in Brazil, only some of whom appear in this story. The list would be much too long to include here. Our lives and our faith experiences have been eternally blended. In reality, this is their story, not mine. I just had the privilege of being in the right place at the right time.

Once I began writing, it became apparent that I needed blocks of time in isolation from my day-to-day reality in order to reconnect with the past. On numerous occasions my brother Loren and his wife,

Marge, allowed me to set up shop with file boxes, journals, laptop, and a box of groceries in their apartment at the Embarcadero in Newport, Oregon.

Dave and Donna Simonson, in a similar way, allowed me to hunker down in the Hillside Lodge at their Falls Creek Retreat Center near Raymond, Washington. The staff did their best to make me comfortable but could do nothing to stop the distraction of deer walking by my window. Falls Creek is an extraordinary place.

A special thank you to Jake and Marge Barnett and to George and Marilyn Duff for the creative and compassionate ways they have cared for and encouraged us.

Words are inadequate to express our gratitude to the pastors, staff, and many friends at Mercer Island Covenant Church. Your warm welcome embraced us as a family when we most needed to feel accepted and loved. Your generosity provided for us when we most needed financial support. Your prayers sustained us when we faced difficult times. You are a vital part of our story in Brazil.

For almost as long as I have known him, Chuck "Monte" Unger has urged me to write. I like to think that the wonderful days Chuck and I spent together in Brazil in 1976 ignited a small flame that became a blazing fire when I started this project.

Karen Lee-Thorp encouraged me as a writer and came to my rescue when I needed fresh motivation.

Hugh Steven is a historical biographer with Wycliffe Bible Translators and the author of more than thirty-two books, including a three-volume work on the life and times of Wycliffe founder William Cameron Townsend. In one of our initial conversations he responded to my remark that I was uncertain if what I was writing would ever get published: "You write history because it is history." I repeated that phrase to myself more than once when I wondered if I was wasting my time.

The crew at NavPress have been exceptional in their efforts on this project. Tia Stauffer worked through the manuscript and helped me clean up some of the more convoluted sections. Whatever you find to be unintelligible is my fault, not hers. Don Simpson read my first few chapters and convinced me to keep writing when I wasn't sure that the number of potential readers exceeded the members of my own family. He seemed confident that this was a story that had to be written.

Finally a word of tribute to my wife, Carol, and our three sons, Kent, Daniel, and Brian, who were participants from day one in the story you are about to read. They have each read the manuscript and contributed memories and details. They have provided an abundance of encouragement. But most importantly they have allowed God to be at work in their lives while as a family we lived through the events recorded in this book. As a result, Carol, Kent, Daniel, and Brian each possess an amazing depth of character that is shaped by a worldview that can only come from being immersed in the kind of adventure I have tried to describe in these pages. I love you and am honored to be known as your husband and your father.

Mercer Island, Washington
May 2009

INTRODUCTION

FEIJOADA — MORE THAN JUST A MEAL

IT WAS NOON, Saturday, November 28, 1964, our third day in Brazil. I was in a noisy restaurant in downtown Campinas. Seated next to me was Daví, a young Brazilian whom I had met the day before at the Sears store where he worked. He had invited me to meet some of his friends for lunch. My mind was spinning like a ship's radar, picking up the sights, sounds, and smells.

Waiters in white jackets streamed from the kitchen burdened with platters of rice, dishes of collard greens fried in bacon grease, and steaming clay pots filled with black beans and assorted pieces of meat, including spicy sausage, pig's ears and tail. Plates of peeled orange slices added a dash of color. I was about to be introduced to a *feijoada*, Brazil's national dish.

"Let me serve up your plate," Daví said in his heavily accented English. There was a mischievous twinkle in his eye as he picked up my plate and spooned on a layer of rice. Next he ladled some beans and a few pieces of meat over the rice. He continued stirring the pot, searching, and then deftly placed a final piece of meat in the middle of the plate. At first I couldn't believe my eyes. It was a pig's snout!

As I looked up from my plate, I realized every set of eyes around that table was watching me, including those of my American colleague,

Jim Petersen, seated across from me. Daví completed my plate with a mound of collard greens and an orange slice, and then he filled his own plate in the same way. Meanwhile the rest of the guys were filling their plates, and someone called out *bom apetite*, which was the signal to begin eating. I lifted a forkful toward my mouth, not knowing what to expect.

That day, that restaurant, that table filled with young Brazilians, and that steaming plate of feijoada—it was more than just a meal; it became something of a cultural continental divide. I was crossing over into a whole new world, leaving behind all that was familiar and comfortable. It was the beginning of an adventure that was to profoundly affect every area of my life, including my understanding of the gospel and my relationship with God.

That first mouthful of feijoada set off an explosion of new tastes in my mouth. The beans, the meat, and the spices had simmered for hours, creating a rich dark sauce that blended with the rice. The beans, rice, and collard greens combined into a unique culinary experience that I have never forgotten. Even now as I write these words, I salivate, thinking about the taste of a feijoada. It's a calorie-counter's worst nightmare, but if you are curious, you can find a recipe for feijoada on the Internet.

However, if you want the real thing, you will have to travel with me to Brazil, gather with a few of my friends around a table on a Saturday afternoon, and let one of them serve up your plate.

In the meantime, turn the page, and travel with me as I tell you stories of what life was like in Brazil. I'll describe some of the things we learned, introduce you to a few of our fascinating Brazilian friends, and take you along on some of our wonderful adventures of leaving the crowd behind and crossing over to the other side of the lake.

In the process you may discover that God wants to open up some new relationships with people who are not part of your normal traffic patterns, people who rarely, if ever, show up at your church and have little or no interest in what goes on there.

PART ONE

1964–1968

CHAPTER 1

PRAYING ON THE PEOPLE STREET

WE THREADED OUR way through the nighttime crowds on Curitiba's "people street." As Jim and I walked, we looked into the faces of the men, some standing in the coffee bars, others gathered in circles engaged in animated conversation. And we prayed.

"God, those are the kinds of men we want to see come to faith in Jesus."

"Lord, we want to find ourselves in a circle like that talking about your kingdom."

It was December 1964. The Lottis and Petersen families were celebrating their first Christmas together in Brazil, which was also something of a reunion. Eleven years earlier, in the fall of 1953, Jim Petersen, Marge Pyne, Carol Bauer, and I were all living in Minneapolis. Jim was an art major at the University of Minnesota. Marge, Carol, and I were studying at Northwestern College and would frequently sit together in class or in the student cafeteria. Carol and Marge had part-time jobs in the same hospital.

Jim and I were part of a group of guys who liked jazz and would attend Jazz at the Philharmonic concerts. I had my initial involvement with The Navigators during those years. Jim and Marge were married in July of 1954 while they were both still in college. After Carol and

I graduated, we wound up working together with The North America Indian Mission in British Columbia, Canada. We became engaged and were married in October of 1958.

In 1960 we left the mission in Canada, reconnected with The Navigators, and started a student ministry on the campus of Northern Illinois University. That's where we were when we learned that Jim and Marge were preparing to move to Brazil and that we were on Jim's "list" to join them.

So when the four of us, along with our five children, gathered around that Brazilian Christmas tree in 1964, we were very aware that this was no coincidence. God had something special planned for us.

Jim and Marge, along with their daughter, Michelle, age three, had arrived in Brazil in August of 1963. They settled temporarily in Campinas to begin language study. During the year that they were in school, Jim began to survey different cities where we might launch our ministry among university students. He began receiving advice from Brazilian pastors and other missionaries regarding the campus environments. The essence of what they were saying was, "Attempting to reach students is a waste of time. Students are very politically oriented and will not be interested in discussing the Bible with North Americans." It was apparent we were on a collision course with these widely held opinions. This raised the question, Were we being foolish to ignore this advice?

To further complicate things, in March of 1964, years of political tension erupted into an armed revolution. The civilian government was replaced by a military dictatorship, setting off harsh repression of some of the defeated political factions. Rumors circulated that the U.S. Navy had been off the coast of Brazil, ready to lend support to Brazil's armed forces. While the military intervention turned the country away from a possible takeover by the Brazilian Communist Party, it also raised the level of anti-American sentiment among university students to new heights. We learned the significance of that the moment we set foot on a university campus. We were operating under a sinister cloud of suspicion that we were CIA agents.

Jim described what happened in the course of that year based on notes from his journal dated August 1964:

After our year in language school, Marge and I took a break and went to Guarujá beach. I was struggling with the apparent absurdity of what we were doing. Here we were, a man with a pregnant wife and a three-year-old daughter, in a country of 100 million people. What madness led us to believe our presence would make any difference to anyone or anything?

I had been reading in the book of Isaiah and on that day found myself in Isaiah 45. In it, God addresses the Persian king Cyrus and says,

> *I will go before you and will level the mountains; I will break down gates of bronze and cut through bars of iron. I will give you the treasures of darkness . . . so that you may know that I am the LORD. . . . I will strengthen you . . . so that from the rising of the sun to the place of its setting men may know there is none besides me. . . . I will raise up Cyrus in my righteousness: I will make all his ways straight. He will rebuild my city and set my exiles free, but not for a price or reward, says the LORD Almighty.*
>
> *This is what the LORD says: "The products of Egypt and the merchandise of Cush, and those tall Sabeans—they will come over to you . . . coming over to you in chains. They will bow down before you and plead with you, saying, 'Surely God is with you, and there is no other; there is no other god.'" (verses 2-3,5-6,13-14)*

As I read this, I thought, *This is what we need God to do for us. We need him to cut a path through all these obstacles that loom before us, to straighten out our road. We need him to bring people to us, able people who are engaged in the affairs of this country.*

But, unfortunately, this was not written to me; it was written to Cyrus, a Persian king who lived some 2,600 years ago. I put my Bible away.

Three days later this passage was still roaring around in my head. I thought, *If God wanted to say something to me today, how would he do it?* Would I hear a voice coming out of the wall? That was doubtful. Or, would the Holy Spirit call my attention to something he had already said in a different time and place, and tell me, "What I told Cyrus through Isaiah is what I am telling you today." That would be more likely.

Was I being subjective? Yes, of course I was. Was I conjuring up something that wasn't really happening? Of course I could have been. Only time would tell. Galatians 3:29 helped me at this point: "If you belong to Christ, then you are Abraham's seed, and heirs according to the promise." I felt the freedom to accept this Isaiah passage as God's personal word to us.

The effects were immediate. In the next days I wrote in my journal,

> *God has prepared people for us and he will bring them to us. . . . I am looking forward to the future because the results have already been assured. Men of stature with prepared hearts will be given to us. To have a promise like this is like reading the last chapter of a mystery first. You not only know if it will work out, you know how.*

Recently, in looking back to those experiences, Jim reflected on their significance during our initial years:

This chapter in Isaiah has been a guide for us over these succeeding 40 years in many ways. It has defined our sphere of ministry and kept us on track. This is the only time in our lives God used a passage of Scripture to direct us in this way. The immediate application was obvious; we were to go to people in chains. That means people who are captives in Satan's dominion, the lost. They were to be our starting point.

Obviously, if one wants to inherit a promise, one must be obedient to it. This distinction narrowed our options to a single conclusion; our starting point must be among lost people, people who were not already within the community of the church.

Four months after Jim wrote those words in his journal, in the evenings of that holiday season after our five small children had been fed, bathed, and bedded down, Jim and I would drive into downtown Curitiba to walk the streets and pray. The words from those verses in Isaiah 45 emboldened us to pray for the kind of people described as "the products of Egypt and the merchandise of Cush, and those tall Sabeans." We weren't sure what that meant, but we soon found out as God began to answer those prayers.

Ken Lottis and Jim Petersen pause for a cafezinho in one of Curitiba's ubiquitous coffee bars on the "people street."

CHAPTER 2

SPEAKING THE LANGUAGE, UNDERSTANDING THE CULTURE

DRIVING ON THE main highway between Curitiba and São Paulo, designated as BR-116, was an unforgettable test of nerves that required a special blend of skills, something in between those of a Formula One race car driver and a Las Vegas gambler. It was four hundred kilometers of two narrow lanes of asphalt, with an endless assortment of potholes. Long lines of heavily loaded trucks belched black diesel exhaust as they crawled up winding mountain roads. The big interstate buses often served to run interference when passing those long lines of trucks. Last but not least were the challenges of dodging horse-drawn carts, people on bicycles, and the occasional cow or horse that wandered onto the highway.

Shortly after New Year's Day of 1965, Jim loaded us into his Vemaguet (a German-designed, Brazilian-built mini–station wagon with a fifty-horsepower, three-cylinder, two-cycle engine that sounded like a lawn mower on steroids), and we headed out onto BR-116 for the trip back to Campinas. Seven hours later we breathed a sigh of relief when we pulled into the driveway of our little rented house on Rua Barbosa da Cunha, No. 614.

On Monday, January 11, we started classes at the language school. The first thing they taught us to say was, "*Barbosa da Cunha, seiscentos e quatorze*," which was our address. That critical information allowed us to make purchases at the markets, step into one of the hundreds of well-maintained taxicabs in the city of Campinas, give the driver that address, and hope that he didn't try to carry on any further conversation.

I attended classes in the morning, Carol in the afternoon. Kent, at four years and nine months, began attending nursery school in the afternoons. It was embarrassing, but his language learning quickly accelerated past his parents. A month later, after Daniel's third birthday, he joined his brother at the nursery school's afternoon sessions. Sixteen-month-old Brian stayed at home under the loving care of Lourdes, the fourteen-year-old Brazilian girl who worked as our maid.

On January 21, I wrote these words in my journal: "Eight days into language school. It has been a rapid introduction, and the progress has been encouraging. The new sounds of the language are becoming more familiar to ear and tongue. But there's a long way to go."

Little did we know at that point just how long that "way" really was. Someone has said, "Before you can master another language, you have to murder it." During those initial months we became merciless assassins of Portuguese. Even something as simple as buying bread and milk at the corner bakery had the potential to produce a chorus of giggles from the teenage girls who waited on us. After one such face-reddening experience, I asked Jim, who was with me, why they were laughing. With a grin he replied, "You asked for a *pau suja*, 'a dirty stick,' instead of *pão de soja*, 'soy bread.'"

The language-learning system employed at the school was excellent, using state-of-the-art phonetic techniques for teaching pronunciation, syntax, and grammar. Classes were intentionally small, with three or four students per teacher, and as students progressed through the yearlong course, there was more individual one-on-one tutoring.

But learning a language must be accompanied by learning the culture. In addition to what I was learning at the school, I had the advantage of the friendships that Jim Petersen and Harry MacDonald, of Young Life, had developed while they were in Campinas. They had spent a lot of time with the group of young men I had met at the feijoada. Now they had moved—Jim to Curitiba and Harry to São Paulo—leaving me to enjoy the benefits of these relationships.

My journal entries casually reflect the early involvement with these young men.

January 31: Quite a day. . . . I went with Daví (and friends) to a "futebol" game. There was a huge crowd, and the game was very rough and dirty—worst I've seen so far. The game ended with a swarm of fans vaulting the fence and getting on the field. In seconds a handful of fights had broken out between players and spectators. . . . As Daví and I started out of the stadium, we got involved in a mass stampede. . . . Like I said, quite a day.

March 6: Had Luiz over last night for dinner, chess, and music. I find it difficult to communicate with this guy. . . . This noon Orlando was here. Had a good time with him. Some time in English, but mostly in the Word in Portuguese.

March 15: Orlando was here again. It was a good time.

In addition to this kind of personal involvement, once a week Harry and Hope MacDonald would make the hour and a half drive from São Paulo to lead a lunch-hour Bible study in our home. These were our first opportunities to entertain Brazilians in our home, which was another dimension of learning the culture. The food itself was simple enough. A typical lunch included rice and beans, a small piece of beef somewhat like a minute steak, and a leaf of lettuce with a few slices of tomato. Unable to find salad dressing at the corner grocery store, Carol created a blend of mayonnaise and ketchup that the Brazilians, much to her consternation, spooned onto their rice. But the biggest challenge was to brew coffee that suited their tastes. Her initial attempts were laughingly labeled as *agua de batata*, meaning "the water left over after you've boiled potatoes."

It was only later that we fully appreciated the value and significance of what we were learning from these experiences. Most of the cultural orientation being taught to the missionaries in the classrooms at the language school focused on adaptation into the evangelical subculture of the Protestant church in a country that was more than 90 percent Roman Catholic.

Our orientation, by comparison, was taking place in real-life contexts of relationship with these young Brazilian friends. These were individuals who had been raised as Catholics but in their early teen years had abandoned any meaningful affiliation with the church. We defined them as being "cultural Catholics," in that being Brazilian was almost synonymous with being Catholic. They would use a phrase in Portuguese to describe their Catholicism: *Sou católico de boca para fora!* which translates "I am a Catholic from my mouth outward." This phrase was often accompanied by a gesture, pointing to one's throat and adding, *A coisa não desce mais*, meaning "I can't swallow that stuff anymore."

The result was evidenced in a very secularized worldview, which in effect declared the Catholic Church, and religion in general, to be irrelevant to modern life. They were atheist or agnostic in their beliefs and in some cases had adopted Marxist political views. Having bailed out of one religious system, there was little or no interest in joining another, such as a traditional Protestant denomination.

These friendships and these experiences were in a sense a preview of coming attractions. In the years ahead we would be tapping into a generation of young people who would be responsive to the claims of

Jesus Christ on their lives but who would shun any affiliation with the institutional church.

At the time, these experiences were moving us into uncharted territory with few precedents to guide us. There were nagging unanswerable questions about what we would do with people who would respond to the person of Christ but would not make the transition into a traditional church. Now it seems commonplace to find people curious about spirituality but disinterested in attending a traditional church. But in the mid-1960s it was all new for us.

CHAPTER 3

MORE LANGUAGE, MORE CULTURE

IN THE WEEKS and months that followed, I established something of a routine that kept me in touch with Daví and some of the other guys who had shared that memorable feijoada. They became good friends and, unbeknownst to them, my cultural mentors. Whenever I had a break from my language classes, I would hop on an old streetcar that passed near our house and ride downtown. When I would arrive at Daví's place of work, he would greet me with an *abraço*, a back-slapping, rib-cracking hug, and then say *vamos tomar um cafezinho*, "let's go have some coffee."

We would grab one or two other guys on our way out of the store, walk around the corner to their favorite coffee bar, and begin the little ceremony connected to the *cafezinho*, meaning "the little coffee." First we'd have a dispute as to who paid. Next it was who would put the sugar into the small demitasse cups, filling the bottom third of the cup. The losers would show their disdain for the amount of sugar by removing a tiny amount with a spoon and depositing it on the saucer. The waitress would fill the cup with blazing hot liquid that seemed to possess the color and consistency of tar. As we sipped the very sweet black coffee, I would try out my latest acquisitions in Portuguese, which always seemed to provide entertainment for my circle of friends, the other customers, and the waitresses behind the counter. But as I rode the streetcar home, I was encouraged by the affirmation those coffee-drinking sessions provided.

On Saturday or Sunday afternoons I would frequently join Daví and his friends to go to a *futebol* (soccer) game. I would sit with them on concrete bleachers in the scorching afternoon sun, cheer for their team, and heckle the officials. I quickly learned that, like any sport, futebol in Brazil has its own vocabulary.

While sitting in those bleachers, I was acquiring a vocabulary that was not being taught to the missionaries at the language school. I became aware of that one Monday morning in class when the teacher, a saintly older Brazilian lady, asked the students what we had done over the weekend and if we had learned any new words.

First she was scandalized that I had gone to a futebol game on the Lord's Day, then horrified as I proudly repeated the words that my friends had shouted throughout the game. She directed me to speak to one of the male instructors, from whom I learned that those words were a very offensive and obscene remark about someone's mother.

Often after a game the guys would take me along to a tiny bar a few blocks from the stadium where we were served mouthwatering barbecued chicken from a charcoal-fired rotisserie. The chicken was accompanied by french fries, rice, and a salad, which the guys washed down with bottles of cold beer.

The first time we did this, an argument ensued on the sidewalk as we exited the bar. It was apparent, from the repeated glances in my direction, that the discussion had something to do with me. A settlement was reached, and each of the guys said good-bye, accompanied by a big abraço.

"What was that all about?" I asked Daví, in English, as we walked toward my streetcar.

I will never forget his reply. "They're heading out to a brothel. They wanted to invite you along and were afraid you would be offended if I didn't at least ask you. I tried to explain to them you wouldn't be interested."

As I rode the streetcar home that night, it sunk in that I had never had a group of friends like these guys. I was in a new country, learning a new language, and trying to understand a new culture. But even more overwhelming was the realization that these new friends were the kind of men described in those verses in Isaiah 45, "coming over . . . in chains." In this case the chains were patterns of behavior considered so normal that their consciences were concerned only that I would be offended if they didn't invite me to go with them to a brothel.

CHAPTER 4

BIG BUCKS AND BIG SHOES

THE INITIAL MONTHS in Brazil pushed us into an accelerated period of learning, unlike anything we had ever experienced before. Our learning curve simply went vertical in so many different areas of everyday life! Like money.

In mid-December of 1964 the exchange rate for the Brazilian cruzeiro was Cr$1,630 to US$1. The largest denomination in the currency was a Cr$5,000 bill, worth about US$3.06. Think about that. You can easily carry $100 in a billfold or purse with five $20 bills; I needed thirty-three of those $5,000 cruzeiro bills.

There were bills worth $1,000, $500, $100, $50, $20, and $10 cruzeiros. Do the math. Fifty U.S. dollars cashed into cruzeiros was $81,500, a sizeable bundle! An ordinary wallet like I carried in my hip pocket in the United States was not up to the task of carrying this much currency. Like other Brazilian men, I began carrying a small leather purse about the size of a typical hardback book.

Making change was a nightmare. Until we could understand all the numbers in Portuguese, we would simply hold out a handful of money and trust the merchant or the taxi driver to take the needed amount.

My first purchase in a retail store was an umbrella that cost Cr$9,250 or US$5.65. My first haircut cost me Cr$500, or about twenty-eight cents. One of those tiny cups of coffee was about three cents. Riding the streetcar cost me about two cents.

For the first time in our six years of marriage, we began buying new furniture. We quickly learned that prices on furniture and appliances were not fixed. Because of the rapid rate of inflation, a price quoted in the morning would usually be higher by afternoon.

We immediately purchased a propane kitchen stove, a refrigerator, a washing machine, a box spring and mattress, and several other items from the same store. Rather than pay cash, I signed a promissory note, due in thirty days.

By the time that note came due, fellow missionaries had familiarized me to the process for changing U.S. dollars into Brazilian cruzeiros. There were a variety of independent money-changing businesses, euphemistically called the "parallel market," in addition to the official exchange desks in the banks. These businesses were at times tolerated by the government; at other times they were closed down. For the first six months we were in the country, we used the parallel market.

On the day I had to pay off the promissory note, I went to a money changer who operated out of a real-estate business. I stepped up to the counter and said only a single word, *cambio*, the word for "exchange." The man behind the counter recognized me and pressed a button under the counter; the door to my right buzzed, allowing me to enter a small office where a man was seated behind a desk working several telephones simultaneously. I held up the check from my bank in Colorado Springs for him to see the amount. He spoke into several telephones and then scribbled an exchange rate on a scrap of paper. I nodded okay. He pulled his checkbook out of a drawer and wrote a check for well over Cr$1 million. We exchanged checks, shook hands, and I was out the door leaving him still working the phones; we had completed the Cr$1 million transaction with one word, a nod, and a handshake.

Minutes later I entered a bank and presented the check to be cashed. I waited and watched the check as it moved from desk to desk, gathering initials before it was returned to the teller. He then began piling rubber-banded bundles of money on the counter. These bundles, about two inches thick, were comprised mostly of $500 and $1,000 cruzeiro bills with an occasional $5,000 bill. Having been precounted and banded, only the bundles were counted as the teller pushed them through the wicket in my direction. Overwhelmed, I hadn't the slightest idea if he was giving me the correct amount of money. Not wanting to create a scene, I simply opened my attaché case and managed to get all the bundles in. I felt like I was pulling off a bank robbery!

Nervously I turned toward the door, wondering if my transaction had attracted the attention of a would-be thief. I hurriedly walked several blocks to the store, where I handed over the promissory note. I unloaded the money from my briefcase and watched in amazement as the cashier only counted the bundles. He then stamped the promissory note as paid and handed it back to me.

Another area of adjustment, particularly for Carol, was grocery shopping. Supermarkets would not make their appearance in Brazil for another decade. Milk and freshly baked bread were purchased daily from a nearby corner bakery. At the same busy intersection there was a small butcher shop offering a selection of fresh beef, pork, and chicken.

Fresh fruits and vegetables were purchased from street markets that set up once a week in our neighborhood. Carol would walk through the market pulling a small two-wheeled cart and carrying several large shopping bags. Merchants would call out their prices, and Carol learned to do some good-natured bargaining to get more for her money.

The learning curve included things about the language that went beyond correct pronunciation, verb conjugation, and sentence structure. For example, we were given a class in profanity and discovered to our horror that both Kent and Daniel had already learned some of these words while playing with children in the neighborhood.

We learned that, just as in English, there are things people say in Portuguese that they don't mean. It is common to greet someone with "How ya doin'?" without expecting a detailed health report as an answer. If a Brazilian is saying good-bye and adds the phrase *aparece lá em casa*, which literally means, "show up at the house," that does not constitute an invitation to visit his home.

Then there are the little ceremonies we go through when saying hello and good-bye that have a new set of cues that must be followed. When two men who are friends meet on the street, they greet one another with an abraço, a hug that involves body contact and some backslapping. If two women who are friends meet, they exchange a series of kisses on both cheeks. Knowing which cheek to start on is essential to avoid an embarrassing nose-to-nose collision. Greetings between men and women take on a far more complicated set of variables, depending on how well they know each other. Do I just shake the lady's hand, do I exchange kisses, or is a hug in order? There's no simple answer, and if you get it wrong, it can be very embarrassing or even offensive!

Walking the downtown streets of Campinas, I quickly learned there were things that identified me as an American. Like my brand-new pair of Florsheim Wing Tips given to me just a few days before we left the United States. The shoeshine boys could spot them half a block away and greeted me with cries of "Shine, meester?" I bought a pair of Brazilian shoes, put away the Florsheims, and never wore them again.

One day as Jim and I were finishing a cup of cafezinho, we watched two Mormon missionaries walk past. We agreed that they were easily identified by their white shirts, ties, and big American shoes. But there was something else. It was the way they walked. We wondered, *Do we walk that way?* We came up with a way to find out.

We stood in a nearby doorway until we spotted two Brazilian men walking toward us. As they passed, we stepped in a few yards behind them and began to match their pace, step for step. It was amazing. We had to adjust the length of our stride, or we would have quickly overtaken them. Plus, our pace was too fast, and we had to force ourselves to slow down. From that day on, Jim and I made it a habit to periodically step in behind a man who was about our height and "recalibrate" our style of walking in an effort to be more like a Brazilian.

There is so much to learn when you move into a new culture, so much more than just learning to speak the language. Day-to-day things like changing money and paying bills, buying bread and bananas, saying hello and good-bye, and, yes, even what kind of shoes you wear and how you walk.

Our goal, of course, was to immerse ourselves to the greatest possible degree in the Brazilian culture and way of life. It would simply not be enough to stand on a street corner or in an auditorium and proclaim a message in grammatically correct, accent-free Portuguese.

Rather we needed to shed as much of our American culture and lifestyle as possible and incarnate the gospel of Christ in the way we lived our everyday lives.

In Philippians 2:7-8 Paul very succinctly described this process that Jesus went through and modeled for us: "But [he] made himself of no reputation, and took upon him the form of a servant, and was made in the likeness of men: And being found in fashion as a man, he humbled himself, and became obedient unto death, even the death of the cross" (KJV).

Ken, Carol, Dan, Kent, and Brian all dressed up for an outing in downtown Curitiba (1966).

CHAPTER 5

KEYS TO A HOUSE AND KEYS TO THE KINGDOM

WE WERE INTO the final weeks of language study and making preparations for the 360-mile move from Campinas to Curitiba. The first week of November the telephone, which sat silent for days at a time, startled us when it began ringing.

"I've found you guys a house. But you're going to need a *fiador*." It was Jim, yelling at the top of his lungs over a bad long-distance connection from Curitiba.

He went on to explain the common practice in Brazil of requiring a fiador, a cosigner to a rental agreement who owned property in the same city. Fortunately, one of my teachers in the language school had a cousin who lived in Curitiba, and her husband agreed to be my fiador.

Several weeks later, carrying a letter of introduction, I walked into the factory of Luciano Bocatto, a short, barrel-chested Italian immigrant who had come to Brazil right after World War II. His business employed 120 people to make pasta (macaroni, spaghetti, etc.) that was distributed over a wide area by a fleet of twenty trucks.

He enfolded me in a bear-hug embrace, ushered me into his cramped office, and served me a cafezinho from a thermos. We quickly handled the legal details required by the homeowner to verify that he was qualified to sign as my fiador. As we shifted to family issues, he began suggesting all the things we could do together with our boys.

Once we moved to Curitiba, our friendship began to develop. In a letter I described it this way:

> The first time I visited in his luxurious home he called me *reverendo* and served me orange juice. When he found out I wasn't a pastor, he called me *senhor*, which is more common yet respectful. Now he calls me *você*, which you use with just your friends, and he serves me his favorite wine. Recently he told me, "Ken, the desire to make money with my business no longer attracts me, the desire to have a big car no longer attracts me, the desire to have a woman no longer attracts me. . . . The only thing that interests me now is something spiritual . . . spiritual reality."

My relationship with this man served as further confirmation that we were surrounding ourselves with people who, while having no meaningful connection to or interest in the church, were spiritually hungry. Luciano responded to the notion that he could sit in my living room with a group of university students, sip a cafezinho, smoke his cigarettes, and discuss a passage from the Bible.

The second observation that I drew from my friendship with Luciano came from that difficulty in what title to use when he spoke with me. I wasn't an ordained minister, so the reverendo title didn't fit. I didn't wear the kind of clothes that would identify me as a business-man, nor did I use the more formal, polished Portuguese of a lawyer or politician, so the word *senhor* was not appropriate. Thus after our initial conversations he began using the familiar *você*, which is used between family members and friends.

This absence of identifying structure created a problem, which I will describe in a later chapter. But it also worked to our advan-tage. Many young Brazilians who had been raised in a hierarchical and authoritative religious structure had learned early on that certain questions should not be asked and statements of doctrine should not be challenged. Those were the very questions and issues we welcomed and from which we often introduced a student to the Scriptures.

Initially, as I was still acquiring additional vocabulary in Portuguese, rather than trying to frame my own answer, I would ask myself, *Where can I find a passage in the Bible that will address this issue?* I would have the student read the passage, and then I'd ask, "What does that say, and how does it help to answer your question?" Rather than getting the impression they were being indoctrinated into some weird North American religious sect, I was giving them answers straight from the Bible.

The major defining religious structure in Brazil is the Roman Catholic Church. Being the largest Catholic nation in the world, located on a predominantly Catholic continent, sharp lines have been historically drawn separating Protestants into a minority. As we sought to define ourselves, we turned to the Scriptures, and it was as if, having removed our North American evangelical lenses, we began to see the kingdom of God on the pages of our Bibles.

The defining structures of the kingdom of God rise above the divisive issues of church history. As we began to focus on the kingdom, we were able to avoid being identified with either a Protestant or a Catholic label. We were convinced that whatever God wanted to do in Latin America, he needed disciples, solid citizens of his kingdom. And if we proclaimed and taught the good news of the kingdom, the rest would take care of itself.

Several years later I attended a lecture given in Brazil by Spencer Bower, a missiologist. At the end of his talk I introduced myself and offered to give him a ride to the airport the next morning.

As we pulled away from the curb and began threading our way through rush-hour traffic, I launched into a series of stories to describe what we were doing. At the airport I continued to talk as he stood in line at the check-in counter. We walked out to the departure gate and, finding no place to sit, hunkered down with our backs against a wall.

I finished what I had to say and asked, "So what do you think? Are we okay?"

When he remained silent, I turned and saw tears in his eyes. It was apparent that he was deeply touched by what he had just heard. Finally he spoke, in a near whisper. "He's going to get it built. One way or another, Ken, he'll get it done." He paused. I was puzzled by what he was saying.

Then he looked at me and went on. "It is just as he said to Peter, 'I'm giving you the keys to the kingdom . . . and I will build my church.' Just keep doing what you're doing, Ken. One way or another, he'll get his church built."

The house on Padre Anchieta Street where the Lottis family lived from December 1965 to February 1970. That's our Brazilian-made VW bug in the driveway and us peeking out the window.

CHAPTER 6

FINDING THE THREAD

IN MANY OF the countries where The Navigators sent their first missionaries, they had gone in at the invitation of, or in collaboration with, other missions agencies. The result was that from day one in a new country, the activity of the Navigator missionary would be dictated by the arrangements that had been made. In some cases this would be training counselors for evangelistic crusades; in others it meant translating and distributing Bible study and Scripture memory materials or working in local churches.

This was not the case in Brazil. We were free to find the pathways into the hearts and minds of young Brazilians. At the time, we had no idea what those pathways were or where they would take us.

The expressions used in that passage from Isaiah 45, however, began to take on significance in mapping those paths as Jim and Marge settled into their first year of activity in Curitiba while Carol and I began our language study in Campinas. The imagery of people "coming over . . . in chains" pointed toward the kinds of men we had prayed for as we walked the streets at night.

In contrast, Jim found himself assisting a group of local churches that was organizing a citywide evangelistic crusade. Several young men, after meeting Jim, expressed an interest in working with Os Navegadores do Brasil—The Navigators of Brazil. These were nice young men, members of local churches, seemingly eager to join forces with us. There was just one thing wrong; as Jim described it, "There were no chains."

So what do you do as a foreigner in a city of half a million people to make some initial friendships outside the walls of a protestant church? It's really quite simple: You pray, you get your friends to pray, and then you start looking for "a thread" that will lead you into a network of existing relationships.

In pursuit of such a thread that would take him into the secular world, Jim sought out Osvaldo, brother of one of the young men who was at the feijoada lunch in Campinas. Osvaldo worked in the laboratory of a multinational chemical industry in Curitiba. He had heard from his brother José about Jim and was curious. So when Jim tracked him down, he accepted an invitation to come for dinner. It didn't take Jim long to realize he'd never met anyone quite like Osvaldo. Jim described this process in his journal:

December 23, 1964: Covered the gospel with Osvaldo last night. Used The Bridge. We spent a couple hours at it, sat on the floor with a piece of chalk and my Bible. We worked our way through, verse by verse, with him interpreting each verse for himself as we came to them. I felt the discussion went well, that he really understood the scriptures—until I asked him what he thought.

He looked at the diagram I had chalked onto the floor, looked at me, looked at the floor, and asked, "You came to Brazil to show people that? I don't get it."

Using the simple illustration called "The Bridge" to present the gospel was what we had been doing with students in the United States for years. So we naturally assumed it would work in Brazil. That response from Osvaldo was a wake-up call. Much of our American experience was not relevant in the Brazilian culture.

January 26, 1965: Spent another session with Osvaldo last night. He's one of the most difficult people I have ever encountered — closer to a free thinker than anything. He posed a philosophy, complete with reincarnation and unidentifiable deities. After working our way through a lot of scripture to the contrary, he said, "That's okay; I didn't believe that anyway. What do you think of . . . ?"

January 29, 1965: Another session with Osvaldo last night. We got into John 1. It really hit him. I think he's coming!

March 18, 1965: Osvaldo trusted the Lord last night. Funny, his questions were intellectual. His problem was a sin he didn't know what to do with. And that he could not resolve until Christ was in his life.

Jim picked up another thread early that year as he stood at the counter in a small shop. Jim recorded that experience in his journal:

January 15, 1965: I was in an art store today getting some pictures framed. There was another customer having a diploma from the University of Michigan framed. His name is Henrique, age 21. I asked him about the diploma. His English was flawless, accent free. He's never been to the States, got his diploma via extension. He has a language school here in town, Yazigi. He invited me to his apartment, and we talked some more.

February 24, 1965: Yesterday, over some tea, I explained the gospel to Henrique. His response was startling. He said, "Count me in. Convert me first and then I have a whole school full of people you can work on." It has paid to wait and win my way with him. We have a 10:00 appointment for today to talk more deeply. He obviously doesn't understand what it is that he's so ready to believe in.

Afternoon: I picked Henrique up and brought him to the house. He wanted to know why Marge and I are here. Based on 2 Corinthians 5:19-20, I explained that we are here to draw people to Christ. He liked that. We spent the afternoon together. I took him around to various schools to promote his language school. He couldn't quit talking about his choice to follow Christ. That night he told Francisca (his wife). She was positive.

March 8, 1965: Yesterday I explained The Bridge to Francisca. I can't read her response. Must pray for her!

March 16, 1965: Henrique and I were in the sauna together about ten days ago. He's let me into his business. He had 78 students. He needed 138 to meet his expenses. (I had done the math, but he hadn't.) I asked him if God might be interested in his business. He didn't think so. "Why not?" I asked. "Because my business is personal, it's for me. God wouldn't be interested in that." I challenged that and we prayed — in 130 degree heat. We asked God to bring him enough students for them to make a good living.

Now, 10 days later, God's blessing on the Arnholdts is staggering. The business has boomed. They have 140 students. Francisca is stunned by the response. Henrique is witnessing to his brother, Henir, and his friend, Berardo.

Another set of threads came from a series of lectures given at the Federal University in Curitiba by a Swiss psychiatrist, Dr. Hans Burki. Jim was asked by a representative of InterVarsity Christian Fellowship to translate for Dr. Burki, which brought him into contact with a number of students. One of those was Mario Nitsche, who stayed behind after a lecture to ask several questions and caught Jim's attention. They agreed to meet a few days later to carry on the discussion. Mario had exchanged his Catholic upbringing for a Marxist framework in his early teen years and had begun to read philosophy. He was attracted to Bertrand Russell and exhaustively read his works, selecting "Why I Am Not a Christian" as the replacement for his Catholic Bible.

Another inquisitive student stayed to talk with Jim. Curt Lorenz was from Timbó, a small but highly industrialized town in the neighboring state of Santa Catarina. Typical of many of the German families who had immigrated into southern Brazil in the first half of the twentieth century, the Lorenz family had been very successful. Curt and his brother Hans were studying law and economics, preparing to take over the family's business interests. Raised in the German Lutheran Church, Curt was in the process of jettisoning most of the rigid and restrictive belief system he had been taught. There were still a few nagging questions that he and Jim began to talk about.

Four names: Osvaldo, Henrique, Mario, and Curt. Four threads that led us into extensive networks of friends, family, and relatives. In hindsight it is absolutely amazing to trace the scores of people with whom we were involved in the years that followed to these four people. You will meet some of them as you read their stories in the chapters ahead.

Our North American results-oriented culture permeates our thinking, causing us to look for big numbers, big events, and big deals. As a result we've come to ignore the importance of the individual. We were to learn the incredible value of investing in the life of just one person at a time.

At the beginning of the school year in 1967 there were twelve of us . . . that number sounded familiar. (*Left to right* Front: Walter M., Ken, Onofre, Curt, Osvaldo; Back: Dinho, Nelson, Hans, Henrique, Jim, Renny, Egon)

CHAPTER 7

IDENTITY AND IDENTIFICATION

WE ENTERED BRAZIL with temporary visas and then initiated a process to convert them to permanent visas. At first it seemed to be sort of a freshman-level course in Brazilian bureaucracy, but it got more complicated as time went on.

Without a permanent visa we could not obtain permanent driver's licenses. The temporary driver's license was issued for sixty or ninety days, depending on the whim of the clerk behind the counter. The renewal procedure seemed to change each time. I would stand in a long line, only to be informed that I needed new photographs, which were about the size of postage stamps. Returning the next day with photographs in hand and enduring another long line, I would be told that I needed to pay a fee at the Banco do Brasil.

So it was a cause for celebration when, after being in the country for more than a year, we were finally issued our permanent visas and identification cards, which were similar to the passbooks that banks used to issue for savings accounts. Carrying those *carteiras de identidade* became a habit; like the American Express slogan, we never left home without them.

But another issue surfaced during this same period of time relating to identification that had nothing to do with visas or passports.

Rather, it had to do with how we introduced ourselves to people we met. How were we to identify ourselves to our neighbors, to students, to curious shopkeepers and merchants who wanted to know what we were doing in their country? We quickly learned that being labeled a "missionary" was not an advantage. In fact, in most cases, especially with university students, it was an immediate turnoff.

Imagine how you would respond if a family from some other country moved into your neighborhood or apartment complex and introduced themselves to you as missionaries. What questions would that raise in your mind? You would probably ask yourself, *Is this some new religion they are bringing into our country?* Or *Are they going to try to convert me?* Until you had some answers to those questions, you would not be very interested in anything they had to say to you.

There were a lot of missionaries in Brazil, literally from all over the world! The Mormons were easily identified by the way they dressed. Many protestant missionaries wore dark suits, carried big Bibles, and frequently distributed literature on the streets or preached through electronic handheld megaphones in parks. We didn't fit any of those stereotypes, and that subsequently created another problem.

People thought we were CIA agents.

At first we joked about it. Tongue-in-cheek, Jim asked a visitor from our office in the United States about some large donations from someone named Charles Ivan Anderson, wondering if his initials were CIA.

We noticed, however, that when we met people for the first time, there was an almost palpable undercurrent of suspicion. This was particularly true with students. I was using a Yashica single-lens reflex camera at that time, and I had a simple darkroom set up in the basement of our home. Whenever I used that camera with the long telephoto lens, it must have contributed to my characterization as a CIA agent, getting pictures of potential troublemakers!

Then one morning I went into the American Consulate in downtown Curitiba to pick up some forms that I needed to file my tax return. While standing at the counter waiting for the clerk to bring the forms, the consul came through the office and greeted me with a friendly wave. I didn't really know the man, but we had met at a party hosted by an American businessman. Moments later the clerk returned with the forms and a message: "The consul would like you join him for a cup of coffee in his office."

We chatted over coffee about the weather, our families, and then suddenly he changed the subject. "I understand you and your friend Petersen know a lot of university students. I would be interested in knowing what they are saying about our government's involvement in Vietnam."

I was immediately uncomfortable with the question itself and with the fact that it was being asked in that location. Ironically he was seated in front of a large window through which I could see one of the main buildings of the university, right across the street. I thought sarcastically to myself, *Why don't you get out from behind that desk, walk across the street, and talk to a few students yourself?*

Instead I replied vaguely, "Oh, they are saying about the same things many students in the United States are saying."

Apparently not sensing my reluctance, he stunned me with what he said next. "You know we have several other young missionaries with . . ."—and he named a well-known American church group— "who come in regularly to tell us what they are picking up in their conversations with young Brazilians. I would like to have you think about doing that for us. There would be some compensation, naturally, to make it worth your time."

There it was, my chance to make it official and actually work for the CIA! But my immediate response to him was, "I really wouldn't be comfortable doing that. Many of these students have become my friends, and I would not want to betray that friendship."

That ended our chitchat over coffee. Later Jim and I agreed that we should probably pull out of the foreign social circuit in the city, which included American businesspeople, employees of the U.S.

Government, and other English-speaking people. Contact with those people could easily be misinterpreted as having some questionable connection with business or government.

Another incident that happened about this same time revealed the depth of suspicion and mistrust we were dealing with. One of the students with whom Jim was reading the gospel of John was being hassled by his friends for his contact with Americans. "How do you know," they asked him, "that those guys are not undercover agents for the CIA?" He noticed that if he dropped by our little office when Jim wasn't there, I would brew some coffee, and we'd pick up in the gospel of John where he and Jim had left off.

He began to wonder if perhaps in preparation for our undercover assignment, we had familiarized ourselves with John's gospel alone as the basis for discussions. He devised a scheme to test that theory. Using the Bible Jim had given him, he opened at random to a page in the Old Testament and began reading in 1 Samuel about King Saul consulting with the witch of Endor. *Perfect*, he thought.

A few days later when I came into the office, Jim greeted me. "Mario was here a while ago and came up with a really weird question. He wanted to know if there was anything in the Bible about a witch in a place called Endor. He seemed really surprised when I had him open to 1 Samuel 28 to read the story."

Years went by before we heard Mario's side of the story, when he told us he had concluded that no one would carry a "front" that far! But it was one more example of the cloud of suspicion under which we lived.

As we grappled with this problem, we realized that there was no easy solution. We laughed about the fact that we couldn't very well carry a card that stated, "The Bearer of This Card Is Not a CIA Agent." We agreed that we could only continue to be as open and transparent as possible, and that included inviting students into our homes to get to know our families.

Then on October 12, 1968, a group of terrorists ambushed and assassinated Charles Rodney Chandler, a thirty-year-old Vietnam veteran who was studying sociology in a small private college in São Paulo. He had given several interviews about the war to military personnel and had attracted the attention of terrorists. Years later a Brazilian historian would write that he was killed not because he had done anything wrong but because he was an American. By killing him the terrorists got international publicity for their cause.

A few months after this incident, Jim and I met with a couple of fellow missionaries to prepare contingency plans should anything of this nature happen to one of us. We realized that we were in between the battle lines of a war zone, facing dangers from both sides. Like Chandler, we could attract the attention of terrorist groups who would assassinate us thinking we were undercover agents for the CIA collaborating with the military dictatorship. Or the Brazilian military police and counterterrorist agents might raid a student apartment where we frequently visited. If we happened to be in the wrong place at the wrong time, we would be hauled off to a military base, imprisoned, and interrogated. In many such cases, those people simply disappeared, never to be heard from again, or "died while trying to escape custody," meaning they were tortured to death.

The history of that period is now being written, free of the censorship that controlled the media then. In reading the stories of what happened to hundreds of people, one cannot but be overwhelmed with the sense that we were under divine protection.

Providing an environment for students to dig into the Scriptures became our trademark.

CHAPTER 8

NO EASY DECISIONS

THE UNIVERSIDADE FEDERAL do Paraná (The Federal University of Paraná) is not located on a centralized campus like most American universities. Rather it is divided and separated by departments, or *faculdades*. Thus the agronomy department is across town from the engineering department, while the medical and dental schools are close to the downtown area.

We needed some kind of central location that could serve as a place where we could meet with students. So one of my first tasks after getting settled in Curitiba was to do some scouting for an office.

I found the perfect spot, on one of the major avenues that ran through the heart of the city, Marechal Deodoro, named after the first president of Brazil. It was an old three-story building with a small sporting goods store at street level. A single doorway at the sidewalk opened onto a hallway with a law firm occupying a suite of offices at the rear of the building. Up a flight of stairs and to the left I found two small offices with a connecting door that were vacant.

When I went back downstairs to inquire at the law firm, I was not only able to rent the offices, but I began a friendship with the young attorney who greeted me. The friendship with Carlos Fernando Correa de Castro and his wife, Mara, became one of the highlights of our years in Brazil and endures to this day.

After applying a fresh coat of paint on the walls and hanging curtains on the windows, we moved in a table and some chairs, a sofa, and a couple of desks where Jim and I could work. We subscribed to a couple of newspapers. Probably the most important item, however, was a small table next to a sink that held a hot plate, a coffeepot, a saucepan, and a collection of cafezinho cups and saucers.

Jim and I honed our skills as makers of cafezinho, while simultaneously carrying on conversations with students who dropped by on their way to or from classes. Knowing they could score a free cup of coffee and read a newspaper soon made our little office a popular spot.

We had a locksmith make up keys to the office door, as well as the entry door into the building. Once we established a friendship with a student and had begun to read the Scriptures together, we would give him a set of those keys. Frequently Jim or I would arrive at the office and find several students there, drinking coffee, reading the newspapers, or spending time together reading the Bible.

It was not until later, however, that we realized how important that office was in establishing our identity. In addition to the coffee and the newspapers, it was a safe and convenient place where students could come with their philosophical and religious questions and know they would be welcomed. Discussions ranged far and wide to include issues of economics, politics, morality, and ethics. But ultimately we wound up reaching for the stack of Bibles at the end of the table. Our identity was defined by our familiarity with the Bible and the person of Christ portrayed on its pages.

Along with setting up this office, I began spending my evenings at Henrique's English language school. He gave me a brief orientation to the methods and materials, and introduced me to a class as a substitute for one of his regular teachers away on vacation. That first evening one student hung back to chat after class, using a mixture of English and Portuguese. He introduced himself as José Onofre. We left the school, and he led me down the street to one of those ubiquitous coffee bars.

After a cup of coffee, we returned to the street to continue our conversation. We were soon joined by several other students from the class. As I stood there, surrounded by students, it dawned on me that just a year earlier, Jim and I had walked this same stretch of sidewalk, praying. We had specifically prayed that God would insert us into these groups of young men who gathered to enjoy coffee and conversation. Now, here I was, standing in just such a group, initiating friendships with these young Brazilians.

My contact with José Onofre continued until summer vacation ended and his classes resumed at the university. He showed up at the school to inform Henrique and me that he had a schedule conflict and would have to withdraw from the class. Not wanting to lose touch with him, I invited him to have dinner with our family.

When he arrived that evening for dinner, our three boys greeted him warmly. Having been previously prompted, they seated themselves on the sofa beside Onofre and a stack of their favorite storybooks, in English, of course. With a smile, I informed him that his assignment was to read a few stories to the boys while I helped Carol get dinner on the table. Adding a reminder to the boys to correct any words he mispronounced, I left the room.

Later that evening, after the boys were in bed, Carol served us coffee in the living room and Onofre began to ask some questions about why we had come to Brazil. In response I related the story of my own spiritual journey.

In my journal entry the next morning, dated March 17, 1966, I wrote,

Onofre and I got together last night. A conversation opened naturally for me to tell my story. It was natural and easy. . . . He responded with interest and animation. As we discussed the fact that God had a plan for his life, we read Ephesians chapter 1. This turned his interest on full volume. He's a typical Catholic . . . admitted he'd lost interest in church in the last two years, but still had a lot of unanswered questions.

A few weeks later we began reading John's gospel, looking for answers to his questions. This was to become a common practice: taking young men like Onofre to the Bible, explaining that this was a historical document, the original source of information about the life and teaching of Jesus Christ. We would clarify that our purpose was to understand what the author was saying; they did not have to accept or believe it. Our intent was to focus on a few simple questions: Who was this historical person called Jesus Christ? What did he expect in the way of response from those who heard him? And finally: If Jesus really is who he claims to be, what difference would it make?

In most cases these young people had never held a Bible in their hands, much less read or studied its content. If we said, "Open to the gospel of John," the student would start paging through the Bible, front to back, in a desperate search. To avoid that embarrassment, we would say, "Open to page 112," which in our stack of inexpensive Bibles published by the Brazilian Bible Society, was John chapter 1. That is where Onofre and I started.

I continued to spend several evenings a week at Henrique's language school. He outfitted me with the type of white smock worn by professors. We would sit behind the reception desk as students arrived for their classes, carrying on conversations in English. Sort of a free demonstration of how fluent we were in the language we were teaching! Henrique could, without missing a beat, speak with a flawless American accent and then switch to a British accent.

Those evenings were providing a steady stream of opportunities to meet students. As friendships developed, most often we eventually found ourselves opening the Bible together.

In April I took over another class when one of Henrique's teachers quit. This was a group of about twenty engineering students who were all classmates. They were a lively and fun bunch of guys who regularly invited me along after class for coffee and conversation on the "people street."

One evening the lesson I was teaching included the word *waffle*.

My students had no idea what a waffle was. The rule in class was to never use Portuguese, which in this case would not have been much help as there is no direct translation for the word. I drew pictures on the blackboard of a waffle, tried to explain how a waffle was made, and got nowhere. In desperation I finally suggested, "How would you guys like to come to our house some evening and eat a waffle?"

Free food for a student is an offer that is rarely refused. When I got home that night, I told Carol that I'd invited twenty students over for waffles on Sunday evening. She thought I'd lost my mind. But she quickly rose to the challenge, borrowed a waffle maker from Marge Petersen, and made up a shopping list for the necessary ingredients.

It was an unforgettable evening. Brazilians do not mix sweet and savory foods, so a waffle, drenched in Carol's homemade pancake syrup, while tasty, provoked discussions as to whether or not they were eating dinner or dessert.

After the waffles were all consumed, the guys were in our living room listening to music. Some played chess, a raucous card game got started, and others looked at books and magazines. That's when one of the students, Nelson Lopes, started paging through a Christmas edition of an *Ideals* magazine. I was standing nearby, so he turned to show me a page and asked, "Is this a quotation from the Bible?"

"Yes, it is from the Old Testament book of Isaiah." It was past midnight when I recorded in my journal what happened next:

> May 29: As we looked at it, he began to talk about his interest in reading the Bible and the difficulty in finding people interested in discussing it. I told him of my contact with Onofre, my study with him, and invited him to join us. He eagerly accepted.

The next week when we met at the office with Onofre, Nelson began by saying, "My father is a Catholic, and my mother is a Lutheran. One of my close friends is Christian Science, and when I am sick, I consult with a spiritist medium instead of a doctor. So I have a lot of questions!"

For the next few months my journal notes documented the hours I was spending with Onofre and Nelson. For a while it was just the two of them. Then Onofre introduced me to his cousin Palhano and to Mario, one of his hometown buddies. So we backed up and started over again in John chapter 1. Nelson continued to show up at the office for our one-on-one sessions, sometimes bringing along a friend.

On October 24, 1966, after nearly five months of reading the Scriptures and answering his questions, I recorded in my journal: "He finally asked, 'What do I have to do?' I explained, and moments later I prayed and then he prayed. Very freely, very clearly . . . 'I want Christ to enter my life and take over completely.'"

By the end of that year it was clear to us that we had made a dramatic change in the way we did evangelism. There were no quick, easy decisions following a brief presentation of the message using an illustration such as "The Bridge" or "The Four Spiritual Laws." Evangelism was no longer an event but rather a process that extended for months and, in some cases, years.

We were observing that evangelism and discipleship were blended into a seamless process. In many cases we were unable to determine when one ended and the other began. In addition it was evident that the message could not be communicated merely as theological facts. The information needed to be understood in the context of friendship that allowed for them to become a part of our lives.

This meant that our marriage relationships, the way we loved and disciplined our children, our behavior at parties and social events, all aspects of our lives integrated to become an incarnation of kingdom culture.

Even eating waffles.

CHAPTER 9

SUNDAY MORNINGS

IN THE MONTHS prior to moving to Brazil, I did a lot of reading in an attempt to educate myself about the country. Along with books on the history, politics, and economy of Brazil, I soaked up the glowing reports from Christian magazines and missions journals about "the fastest growing church in the world." Naturally I was excited by the idea that we were going to be a part of and contribute to this rapid growth.

Once we were in Brazil, our perception of this "fastest growing church" began to change. It started when I got acquainted with that group of young men over feijoada. For them, the very idea of getting involved with a protestant evangelical church had profound cultural and social implications. It would create tension in a family and in some cases result in alienation. To become a *crente*, the Portuguese word for "believer" many evangelicals call themselves, was to be identified as one who adhered to an arbitrarily chosen, legalistic set of dos and don'ts that were not attractive to young, fun-loving Brazilian university students. There were, for example, rules at that time against attending soccer games and going to movies.

When we moved to Curitiba, we began attending a Presbyterian church located near the center of the city. The pastor was a well-educated Brazilian, and we felt comfortable with how similar it was to churches we had attended in the United States. The order of service followed the same pattern we'd grown up with: "The Doxology" and other familiar hymns with words translated from English to Portuguese, a Scripture reading, an anthem by the choir, the offering and announcements, and the sermon followed by the benediction.

So in March of 1967 when Nelson moved into our basement to begin his senior year at the university, it seemed natural to take him along with us to church the next Sunday. It was immediately apparent that he was very, very uncomfortable with so much that was unfamiliar to him. To further complicate things, it was Communion Sunday. As the ushers passed the trays with the bread and the grape juice, he was ashen faced and perspiring. Thinking he might be ill, I asked if he was all right.

He was very quiet during lunch and went downstairs to his room where he stayed until late afternoon. Carol was making coffee, and I sent one of the boys down to invite him to join us for a cafezinho. As we finished the coffee, he asked a question that I will never forget: "You know that I have committed my life to Christ, and I want to learn all that I can while living with you during my last year of school. But my question is, does living in your home mean that I have to attend that church with you every Sunday?" Realizing the implications of what he was asking, I assured him that, "No, living with us does not mean you have to attend that church."

In the conversation that followed, it was obvious that the very things that allowed us to be comfortable in that church service made him uncomfortable. Stepping into that church was like being transported back to Great Britain and North America. The architecture, the décor, the choir robes, and the design of the pews all reflected the origins of the Presbyterian denomination. For us it was like being home. For Nelson it was all foreign.

A few weeks later, Carol and I had dinner with the pastor and his wife. I had come to greatly respect this man and enjoyed hearing him preach. I related this incident with Nelson and asked for his advice. I recorded his response in my journal the next morning:

The problem you face is difficult. To pull a new Christian out of the Catholic Church creates social and family crises that last a lifetime. At the same time, if he does not leave the Catholic Church, the majority of protestant churches are not ready to receive him. In this case, he has received a lot of love, understanding, and fellowship from you and your small groups which most churches cannot offer. Instead, they may place a system of regimentation upon him which to him is not too unlike that which he just left. . . . It seems to me you need to continue to provide for these new Christians in your small groups, in small communities or families, and not be too concerned about getting them into an organized church.

In his wisdom, this Brazilian pastor had spoken words that were prophetic; this was to be exactly what would take place in the years ahead.

What emerged centered around a word we heard the students using: *turma* (TOUR-mah). A turma is an informal gathering of friends for a specific purpose. Students often assembled in a turma to work on a class project or study for an exam. A man might belong to a turma that met once a month to play poker. Women frequently were in a turma that gathered to work on craft projects. Thus the word *turma* was culturally ideal to identify the loosely knit groups of students who gathered to read the Bible and discuss its relevance to modern life.

Interestingly enough, it would seem that the Greek word *ekklesia*, while translated into English as "church," had a broader, more secular meaning similar to the word *turma*. Luke used *ekklesia* in Acts 19:32, 39, and 41 to describe the unruly crowd in Ephesus.

Over the course of the next few months, our church attendance became more spasmodic as the turma became more of a reality. One example was something we called *estudo aberto*, an "open study." The open study was something we put together in an effort to take advantage of a culture built around relationships. Great value is given to friendship, and it became apparent that as students began to get into the Bible with us, they were talking to their friends about what they were learning. While expressing some interest, many of these friends were not ready to join a small-group study. They had questions to ask and just wanted to check out the environment. Was this a safe place for them to talk about their disbelief and their doubts, or would they have something crammed down their throats?

We tried having open studies on weeknights or Saturdays, but eventually settled on Sunday mornings as the time when the university students did not have other scheduled activities. Planning for the event consisted of compiling a list of names, starting with the men already in a small group or a one-on-one study. Then we would ask, "Who have you been talking to—friends, classmates, hometown pals, girlfriends—that you want to invite to the open study?"

On the Friday and Saturday preceding the open study, we would go over those lists, checking to see who needed transportation. Jim and I would be up early, often picking up several carloads and bringing them to one of our homes. It was not unusual to have to go into rooming houses, dorm rooms, or apartments and get guys out of bed. After the previous night's partying, this was frequently a very challenging task.

Carol and Marge would have spread a table with fresh, hot *pãozinho* (an individual-sized French bread), cheese, cold cuts, and goiabada (thick jam made from guava), along with pitchers of freshly brewed coffee and heated milk. After everyone had arrived and had something to eat, we would gather in the living room spilling onto the floors or leaning against the walls. Some would still be sipping coffee; others had located ashtrays and were smoking cigarettes. The Lottis and Petersen children, five of them at this point in time, would mingle with the students and sit in on the discussions.

The first few times we did one of these, Jim or I prepared a brief presentation on some aspect of the gospel, such as the divinity of Christ, his miracles, the Resurrection. We soon handed this off to some of those who had come to faith, coaching them in their preparation. The talk would last fifteen to twenty minutes, and then the floor would be open for discussion.

These wide-open, no-holds-barred discussions often lasted for more than an hour. There were times when Jim or I would provide an answer, but our role more became one of coaching the guys who were already in the Scriptures with us in how to answer basic questions, use the Bible, and not be argumentative.

After the discussion broke up, students would leave to pursue their day's activities. Some would hang around and join us for lunch. Sometimes a group of guys would head off to a soccer match or a movie. But the topic of that morning's discussion followed them wherever they went, providing conversation for the rest of the week.

Sundays became prime times. Even when we didn't have an open study, a spontaneous gathering of students would often join the family for the day. We might do a Brazilian-style barbecue, watch a soccer game on television, play cards, or engage in long conversations that usually tied into something from the Scriptures and issues going on in their lives.

About every four to six weeks, Jim and I would spend a day in a park overlooking the city. We would go over our lists of names, students with whom we were studying the Scriptures and their friends who had come to an open study. We would talk about each person, sharing thoughts and observations, trying to answer four questions:

- What do they need?
- What do they need now?
- What could be done to meet that need?
- If we did that, how would it look to the people we're trying to reach?

We would finish by praying for them, one by one.

During our session together in May of that year, I brought Jim up to date on what was happening in our relationship with Nelson regarding his hometown fiancée, Gita Bircholz. We met Gita and her parents while visiting Nelson and were impressed with what a vivacious and sweet young lady she was. One evening after dinner in a conversation with Carol and me, Nelson made an interesting observation and a startling proposal. "After living with you for these months, it has become obvious that if Gita and I are to have the kind of marriage we want, she has to understand Christ's message as I do. We were planning on getting married at the end of this year, right after I graduate. Instead of waiting until December, what would you think if we were to get married in July during semester break and live with you for the rest of the year?"

Carol and I were both speechless. The space in the basement was limited, but it would work. We nodded our agreement, based on the approval of Gita and her parents. Privately I was skeptical; I could not imagine that both sets of parents would sign off on such an unorthodox way for a young couple to begin their marriage.

To our surprise, Nelson returned from a weekend at home to report that everyone liked the idea, and they had set a wedding date early in July. What's more, they wanted us to be in the wedding party as witnesses. In the traditional Brazilian wedding ceremony, both bride and groom choose godparents and witnesses, couples who are close friends or who have played a special role in their lives. For us to be chosen was a special honor.

Nelson and Gita were the first of many couples in whose weddings we participated or attended. As they settled into their tiny basement apartment, life in our home took on a new dimension. Our evening mealtimes soon established a pattern. As our three boys—now ages four, five, and seven—finished their meals, they were excused from the table to go play while the grown-ups had their coffee and talk time. They were welcome to climb on a lap but not to interrupt our conversation. Gita learned to mimic, in English, Brian's weary plea as he began nodding off in his high chair: "I'm tired. I can't eat any more." These conversations, as we learned years later, laid a foundation for Nelson and Gita's marriage and journey of faith together.

Tucked into the pages of my journal from that era is a faded four-by-six-inch black-and-white photograph that shows Nelson and Gita, along with Carol, Kent, Danny, Brian, Jim, and ten students. I shot that picture during a weekend retreat at a beach, a two-hour drive from Curitiba. That weekend proved to be significant. Among other things, we reorganized the weekly study groups that met in our downtown office, turning over the leadership to several of the more mature guys.

In the weeks that followed, my journal notes reflected how much easier it might have been to maintain leadership ourselves. But the statement we wanted to make came across loud and clear: This was not "our" thing, it was theirs.

As December arrived, we were in a very real sense beginning a transition time. Jim and Marge left the country just before Christmas to visit family and friends in the United States. They would return in June of 1968, and then it was our turn in August. By the time we arrived back in Curitiba in May of 1969, we were ready to enter a new phase.

Marge Petersen serves up one more cafezinho.

PART TWO

1969–1976

CHAPTER 10

RETURN AND REGROUP

IT WASN'T AN alpine meadow in the mountains of Switzerland. Instead, it was a farmer's pasture in a wooded area tucked into the hills rising above the valley of the Itajaí River in the state of Santa Catarina. In July over winter break we took a group of students into this remote area on a camping trip. We pitched a couple of tents under some tall pine trees and stretched a large tarp over poles to serve as a kitchen. Cooking over an open fire was a challenge. Years later whenever those who were on that camping trip got together, someone would retell the hilarious stories of some of the awful food we prepared.

Our primary recreational activity, other than scouring the woods for firewood, was playing soccer on a rather soggy grassy field near our campsite. Before each game the field needed to be cleared of grazing cows and their "deposits." It was during those games that I was first given the nickname *Aranha Branca* (White Spider) for my developing skills as a goalkeeper and my skinny white legs.

Those days spent camping were part of the transition process that was under way in 1969. The Petersens had been away in the United States for six months, and then we followed with an eight-month visit. During that time we had intentionally handed over many of the leadership responsibilities to the students. That meant it was no longer necessary for both Jim and me to stay in Curitiba. It was time for one of us to move out.

We had already decided that the next place to launch a student ministry was Porto Alegre, capital of the state of Rio Grande do Sul. It was twice the size of Curitiba and more of a political hot spot. Jack and Barb Combs, newly assigned to Brazil by The Navigators, arrived to join the team. They had finished language school and moved to Porto Alegre to get acquainted with the city.

Jack came with us on the camping trip and demonstrated his cowboy skills, from his growing-up years in New Mexico. One afternoon a horse wandered into the campsite. Jack grabbed a piece of rope, improvised a bridle, and quietly talked his way alongside the animal. In a flash he was on the horse's back, riding around the pasture as the guys hooted and hollered.

Later, around the campfire, Jack described his impressions of Porto Alegre, and a discussion followed about starting a student ministry there. Some ideas surfaced as to how we could involve students from Curitiba in the initial process.

A few weeks after that rather moist camping experience, there was another historic gathering in the city of Florianópolis to map out plans for the next few years. Attending that meeting were a young Lutheran pastor named Aldo Berndt, his cousin Jorge Hardt, and a dentistry student, Elísio Eger.

Jorge, nicknamed "Dinho," was a student at the university in Curitiba, majoring in chemical engineering. He had been in one of the first groups of students to begin reading John's gospel in 1966. While home for Christmas that year, he got into a conversation with Aldo and mentioned he was in a Bible study group in Curitiba led by two Americans. Knowing Dinho to be something of a skeptic, Aldo was immediately curious as to what had drawn him into something like this. As Dinho described his relationship with this little group of students and the way they interacted around the Scriptures, Aldo's interest increased. He was particularly intrigued that his cousin was finding the person of Christ but remained free from religious entanglements.

A few weeks later, driven by the awareness that he did not know how to do what Dinho was describing, Aldo sought out Jim in a beach town where he was vacationing. Stimulated by the conversation that took place that day, Aldo returned to Florianópolis determined to make some changes in his ministry. Prior to entering seminary and becoming a pastor, Aldo had graduated from dental school in Florianópolis, had practiced dentistry for several years, and still maintained a small dental office.

Elísio heard about Aldo and decided to get acquainted. As the conversation turned to questions about religious beliefs, Elísio responded to Aldo's invitation, and they began to meet together to read the gospel of John. Now, just a few years later, here they were — Dinho, Aldo, and Elísio sitting together in the same room, talking about participating in a vision to reach students with the gospel of Jesus Christ not only in Brazil but in the rest of Latin America.

After this meeting, Jim wrote in a letter,

> I found myself reflecting on how ridiculous the offer we were making must look. "Join us in what we are doing — no pay, no position, no security. Not even a precedent on this continent to show that it can be done."

In that letter he related that one of the Brazilians had summed up the whole process by saying, "Our decisions cannot be based on our fears. We make this decision on the conviction that this is the need and that it's worth doing, whatever the cost." To which Jim added, "I wonder if the smell of fear doesn't always hang around the school of faith. What if we could have offered salaries to these men? No fear. No faith either. God even prospers us through what we don't have."

, , , , ,

In the early afternoon of Tuesday, September 4, 1969, an event took place that stunned the nation of Brazil and changed the political complexion of the country. While being driven from his official residence to the embassy, which was located in Rio de Janeiro, the American ambassador to Brazil, Charles Elbrick, was snatched from his limousine by a group of urban guerrilla terrorists. The rules and protocols of modern international diplomacy that called for diplomatic immunity had been violated. A near-sacred trust that protected diplomats had been broken. The world had dramatically changed.

This small terrorist cell demanded the publication of their manifesto and, more important, the release of fifteen political prisoners with safe transport to political asylum in Mexico, Chile, or Algeria.

Tension in Brasília, the nation's capital, was already high as, only days before, the governing military dictatorship had replaced a seriously ill president, a former army general. The nation was now led by a junta composed of five high-ranking military officers. This junta faced a crisis of unprecedented proportions with huge international implications.

Prior to this point in time the government had denied, in the national and international media, the existence of any "political prisoners." Now the military leaders not only had to admit to a watching world the existence of political prisoners, they also had to negotiate their release with a virtually unknown group of terrorists whose statements criticizing the government were being read on radio, television, and in the newspapers.

It seemed at the time that the entire nation of Brazil was holding its collective breath while awaiting the latest news from Rio. The mere thought that the terrorists might carry out their threats and that the dead body of the U.S. ambassador could be dumped on a street in Rio sent shivers of fear across the country.

After several days the governing junta conceded to the terrorists' demands, and on Saturday, September 6, the fifteen prisoners were loaded on a military transport plane and flown to Mexico. Once their safe arrival was announced on September 7, Ambassador Elbrick was released on a crowded street in downtown Rio. Ironically, this coincided with celebrations of *sete de setembro*, Brazil's Independence Day.

In the days and weeks that followed, the government's reaction was swift and relentless in its pursuit of these urban guerrilla groups. The participants in Elbrick's kidnapping were tracked down one by one and either arrested or killed.

Having tasted success with the Charles Elbrick tactic, terrorist groups went on to repeat the process, kidnapping the ambassadors of Japan, Germany, and Switzerland. In each case the number of political prisoners released was increased and eventually included those who kidnapped Elbrick. The pattern quickly spread and was used by terrorist groups throughout Latin America and around the world.

Having lived under the suspicion of being CIA agents, we, along with many American businesspeople, feared that we too could become easy targets for this new guerrilla tactic. This weighed heavy on us as we pursued plans for our move to Porto Alegre.

In January as we began house hunting in preparation for the move, an attempt was made to kidnap the U.S. Consul in Porto Alegre, Curtis C. Cutter. A former U.S. Marine, Cutter was driving a large American car when terrorists used a Volkswagen sedan to block a narrow street near his official residence. Rather than stop, he gunned the engine and rammed past the VW; as he sped away, the terrorists raked his car with automatic weapon fire, wounding him in the shoulder.

Overnight, Porto Alegre became an armed camp with state militia and regular army troops patrolling the streets and highways in and out of the city. Rumors also had American FBI and CIA agents collaborating with their Brazilian counterparts in an all-out attempt to locate and arrest any and all terrorist groups.

This was the environment into which we were about to move and begin a ministry among university students.

Camping in the mountains provided times of intense relating, great fun, and barely edible food.

CHAPTER 11

BRAZILIAN UNIVERSITY STUDENT VERSUS *NATIONAL GEOGRAPHIC*

THE YOUNG MAN standing next to me was angry. Really angry. We were both standing at the currency exchange desk in Curitiba's branch of The First National City Bank of New York. I was exchanging a check drawn from my Colorado Springs bank into Brazilian cruzeiros. As I eavesdropped, which given his anger was hard to avoid, I realized his situation was unusually complicated.

He had filled out the form for a subscription to *National Geographic* and then had come to this same exchange desk to purchase a money order in U.S. funds. Regulations required the bank to mail the money order directly to the beneficiary—*National Geographic*, in this case. His subscription form was mailed separately. Months had gone by, and he had never received the magazine. And he was getting angrier by the minute as the exchange cashier explained one more time that there was nothing the bank could do.

Since our return to Brazil in mid-May, I had been praying that God would give me a new friend, someone with whom I could read the Bible. Weeks had gone by, and now it appeared this might be God's way of answering my prayer.

I finished my transaction, picked up my deposit receipt, and stepped alongside Dalby, the angry young man.

"Excuse me. I happen to be a subscriber to *National Geographic*, and I understand what your problem is. Your subscription form and the bank's money order arrived separately in the United States and are stored in a huge computer. You need to write a letter, in English, that the computer operator can understand. I can help you do that."

We stepped away from the exchange desk, and I repeated my offer to help and presented him with my business card after scribbling our home address on the back. He refused to accept it, but his friend, who was with him that day, did. We walked out of the bank, stopped to say good-bye on the sidewalk, and parted company. As they turned and headed up the street, I had no way of knowing if I'd ever see him or his friend again — except for that promise in Isaiah, and the fact that I was standing on a stretch of sidewalk where Jim and I had walked and prayed five years before.

It was only recently that I learned from Dalby what was going through his head that day. Fiercely aligned with the radical mentality among students of that era, Dalby wanted nothing to do with me, a gringo. In his thinking all foreigners were the enemy and should be expelled from the country. There was a good possibility I was working with the CIA and could not be trusted. His friend convinced him that they should check me out anyway: "It could be interesting to get to know this gringo."

Several days later, on a Saturday afternoon, Dalby showed up at our front gate. As he described it in a recent letter, this was enemy territory; he needed to be on guard, careful about what he said.

After introducing him to Carol and the boys, I pulled my tiny Olympia portable typewriter out of its case, rolled in a sheet of paper, and, with Dalby seated next to me on the sofa, began typing the letter to *National Geographic*.

As we were finishing the letter, Carol appeared with a tray of tiny cafezinho cups and saucers, a pot of fresh coffee, and some chocolate-chip cookies still warm from the oven. As if on cue, Kent, Daniel, and Brian arrived from the backyard for cookies and their cups of coffee, which were mostly warm milk with shots of coffee for flavor.

He found this very disarming. *Was it possible that the training received from the CIA included the whole family?* he wondered.

After that interlude, Dalby held up the business card I'd given him in the bank and posed a question, one I'd never heard before. "Os Navegadores (The Navigators), are you some kind of travel agent?" His friend had suggested that perhaps I was some crazy scientist who taught classes in celestial navigation.

Not wanting to immediately jump into the subject of what I was doing in the country, I responded with a chuckle and a question of my own. "No, I'm not a travel agent. Why, are you looking for a travel agent?"

"Yes, I guess I am. I've always wanted to travel to the Amazon." Dalby and his friend wanted to explore that vast area, thus their interest in celestial navigation!

I'd been in Brazil long enough to know that for many young Brazilians like Dalby, the Amazon was similar to what Alaska had been for me when I was his age: a place of adventure that was waiting to be explored, offering great hope of excitement and wealth. And a place of escape for a person wanting to run away from something.

I asked, "So why do you want to go to the Amazon?"

That launched Dalby into a long and detailed description of his life. The focus, however, was on his current set of circumstances. The problem with his subscription to the *National Geographic* paled in comparison. He was studying to be an architect at the local Federal University but struggled to get passing grades. He was in CPOR, the Brazilian equivalent of ROTC, and resented what he considered to be the mindless regimentation and rigid discipline of the army. Somewhere in the middle of all this was a complicated relationship with a girlfriend.

I was still trying to fit all this together when Carol stuck her head into the room to say that she was about to put dinner on the table and that she'd set a place for Dalby. It was another one of those occasions when Carol demonstrated her conviction and commitment to the notion that our ministry in Brazil included our home, our marriage, and our three sons . . . and uninvited guests around our dinner table.

As we were seated, something happened that I did not find out about until I was writing this chapter. Dalby's mind was struggling to process the notion that he had been invited to share a meal with the gringo's family when I asked our son Daniel, age seven at the time, to pray. Dalby listened, never having seen or heard anything quite like this in his life. He was suddenly overwhelmed when he heard Daniel include him in his prayer. He wondered, *How did this child know my name?* But hearing his name in that simple prayer convinced him that he was loved and accepted and safe in our family.

Over dinner that evening Dalby told us about his family. The eldest of five brothers and one sister, he was the first in his family to leave home and enter university. He had been struggling with loneliness in the big city, and sitting with our family around the dinner table was obviously something he enjoyed.

After dessert and coffee, we settled back in the living room to continue our conversation. At some point there was a natural opening for me to tell Dalby the story of my faith journey. He countered with his, and I was surprised to learn that he had attended a small Baptist church with his family. He described his disenchantment with all the rules and regulations as his reason for dropping out.

Kent, Danny, and Brian popped in to say good night, pajamaed and ready for bed. Several hours later I drove Dalby back to the apartment he shared with several other students. By that time he had agreed to begin reading the gospel of John with me. Dalby decided that even though he might be getting mixed up in something weird, these possible enemies, these gringos, had something very precious that he needed to learn more about. He later realized that God had used a child's mealtime prayer to capture his heart and mind.

A few days later he showed up at our downtown office. I brewed some coffee, grabbed two Bibles, and we sat down to begin. As I had done many times before, I explained what we were about to do: "We're reading the Bible as a historic document. You don't have to believe it . . . just understand it and answer the question 'Who is Jesus Christ?' Are you okay with that?"

He nodded, and I continued, "After we've worked our way through the first few chapters, we'll add another question: 'If Jesus Christ really is who he claims to be, what difference would that make for us?' Got it?"

He nodded again, and we opened to John's gospel to read the first fourteen verses. "Okay, first question: Based on what the author tells us in verse 14, who is this Word he is talking about?"

An hour or so later we wound up discussing what John meant in verse 12 with the phrase "to all who received him, to those who believed in his name." We talked about getting together again, set a time, and he walked out the door.

I had no way of knowing if he would ever be back. The only thing I could do was pray—and get a few friends to pray. As I had done before, I wrote to my "pray-ers" a few days later. This was a list of ten or twelve people, including my mother, who had a strong desire to pray for me and Carol. Xerox machines had not arrived in Brazil, so this meant using three or four sheets of thin paper and carbon paper to bang out letters on my portable typewriter to get people praying for Dalby.

The other thing I could do was bring in reinforcements. I recruited another student, Walter, who had come to faith in Christ eighteen months earlier. One evening, a week or so later, with Walter in tow, I went to visit Dalby. In a letter home I described it this way:

We drive up a narrow cobblestone street and park the car. A few doors up the street is a rooming house. A girl answers the door and leads us down a hallway to a door. Dalby opens the door and with a warm smile invites us into his room. He introduces us to his roommates, and his warm smile is in sharp contrast to their cold stares.

I've seen this cold stare before. I know exactly what it means. For behind those inspecting eyes, a mind is asking, *Who is this gringo? What does he want? What is he doing here?*

I introduce Walter to Dalby, and we begin to talk. The main topic was "futebol" and Brazil's victory over Venezuela in the eliminations for the world soccer championship, something most Americans know nothing about. The cold stares have warmed a few degrees.

Dalby mentions that he and his roommates are moving to a new room. I volunteer my services as a mover and the use of our mini–station wagon. They refuse my offer, but I insist, and then a few quick glances serve to communicate that this is no polite offer. So they accept, and I agree to come by at 1:00 the next afternoon.

Dalby walks out to the street with us to say good-bye. Walter takes my cue and invites him to an evangelistic Bible study we are planning. Dalby accepts, we say good-bye, and Walter and I shove off.

When I showed up at 1:00 this afternoon to help make the move, Dalby's roommate almost fainted with surprise. Moments later as he and I struggled through a narrow doorway with an old battered desk, he asked, "Are you really an American?" "Yeah, I am." But now the cold stare was gone, and it had been replaced with a warm smile.

Several months went by, and Dalby remained interested but seemingly unmoved by our time together in John's gospel. Because of his church background, he was more familiar with the Bible. It appeared that this familiarity had somehow inoculated him with some kind of religious immunity that prevented him from being infected by the gospel.

Each time we wound up one of our study discussions and he walked out the door, I knew it could be the last time I would ever see him. He was under no obligation to continue. One evening I found myself looking at the clock, waiting for Dalby to show up. He was late, and I was pacing the floor and praying. A letter describes that evening late in October:

> . . . footsteps down the corridor, the door burst open, and in he comes.
>
> "Hi! Sorry I'm a bit late. Did you wait long?"
>
> "No, I'm glad to see you. I made some coffee while I waited. Want some?"
>
> "Thanks, that's just what I need."
>
> He sips his coffee, then says, "Well, I did it. I decided."
>
> My coffee cup stopped in midair. I wondered, *What did he decide? To quit school? Bail out of the army? To go to the Amazon?*
>
> "Decided what?"
>
> "To invite Christ into my life. I did it, all alone, like you said I could, in my room last Saturday night."

I breathed a huge sigh of relief and pointed him to the table, where we sat to begin talking about the next chapter in John and the next chapter in his life.

Our plans to move to Porto Alegre were under way, so I introduced Dalby to a small group of students who had also recently come to faith and were beginning to study the book of Romans. This was exactly what he needed: a nurturing environment where he could continue to grow.

In December, Dalby completed a major milestone in his life by graduating from his reserve officer training program. His family traveled from their home in the western part of the state to Curitiba for the occasion. This gave us the opportunity to meet his parents, his brothers, and his sister. Dalby's father, a quiet, soft-spoken man, seemed eager to meet this American family with whom his son had been spending so much time. He repeatedly expressed his appreciation for our interest in his son and the encouragement we had been to him.

During that visit, Dalby's sister, Neide, stayed in our home for a few days. That began a long-term relationship that eventually touched many lives. But that's another story!

It was about six weeks later that a letter arrived from a university student in Kalamazoo, Michigan, who was involved in the campus ministry of The Navigators. He had somehow heard about Dalby and wrote to say, "There was one week I really had a desire to pray for Dalby. I believe I spent about a week praying every day for him. A week or two later I heard from you that he made the decision."

Once again I was reminded that what we were seeing happen — young men "in chains" like Dalby coming to faith in Christ — was a fulfillment of that promise and an answer to the prayers of people half a world away. People like this student at Western Michigan University.

CHAPTER 12

INVADING PORTO ALEGRE

THE PLAN WE had mapped out for Porto Alegre called for Jim and his family to move in January of 1970 and, together with Jack and Barbara Combs, open a new student ministry. My role in Plan A was to stay behind in Curitiba and coach the emerging leadership team led by Osvaldo Simões.

That plan made good sense. Jim had been the natural leader from the start. We agreed that it would be difficult for the team to move out of Jim's shadow and take charge. But as we were soon reminded, even the best-laid plans are subject to change. The first wrinkle in Plan A appeared when the Petersens discovered that Marge was pregnant . . . with twins! Her delivery date was January of 1970.

Then Jim Downing came to town. It was a standard procedure that about once a year we would receive a visit from Lorne Sanny, then president of The Navigators, or George Sanchez, who was director of overseas operations. These visits provided invaluable opportunities for us to review what we were doing with these older and more experienced men. This year, Sanny opted to send Downing in his place.

Downing was a larger-than-life figure in The Navigators in those days. And as I write this, he still is, at age ninety-four. In the beginning of his twenty-four-year career in the U.S. Navy, Downing was one of the pre-World War II Navigators. The ship he served on, the *USS West Virginia*, was in Pearl Harbor on December 7, 1941. Downing remained in the navy until 1956 when he retired. He slipped quietly into a highly respected leadership role in The Navigators, headquartered in Colorado Springs.

In the years preceding his move to Brazil, Jim Petersen had become well acquainted with Downing. Jim noted that Downing's office door was always open and that he seemed to welcome interruptions. In those spontaneous conversations, Jim grew to appreciate Downing's wisdom and insight.

My exposure to Downing was more superficial; I saw him as a career naval officer, regimented and militaristic in demeanor. So when he showed up in Curitiba in September of 1969, I really did not know what to expect. Would he lay some heavy navy chain-of-command structure on our rather off-the-wall Latin operation? Would he expect to meet World War II–type Navigators that he was accustomed to working with on board battleships and aircraft carriers?

I was in for a big surprise. In reality, Downing had been quietly running interference for us within The Navigators, and he became a major source of affirmation and encouragement. In the days following his arrival, Downing listened intently as we talked about our plans for the next few years. After hearing us out, he came back with some very astute observations and his Plan B for Porto Alegre.

His plan called for me to open the ministry in Porto Alegre and for Jim to remain in Curitiba to help the local leadership team assume responsibilities and learn to work together.

Downing's visit that September was of great encouragement to me personally. One conversation toward the end of his visit illustrates this. During a late-afternoon walk around our neighborhood, he startled me by saying, "I imagine you find it difficult sometimes to work with Petersen."

I wondered if he was a mind reader as he continued without waiting for my response. "I found it very difficult at times to work with

Dawson Trotman [the founder of The Navigators]. I often found myself pouring cold water on his ideas and plans. I think you have a similar relationship with Jim. And he needs to have you to provide balance. So don't get discouraged. You have an important role in your relationship with Jim."

Once we switched to Downing's Plan B, Carol and I began thinking and planning for the move. As parents, one of our first concerns was a school for the boys. In Curitiba they attended Colégio Martinus, named after Martin Luther, which gives a pretty strong hint as to the school's religious affiliation. The principal at Colégio Martinus suggested we check out Colégio Farroupilha in Porto Alegre, which was also affiliated with the Lutheran Church. When we made our first trip to Porto Alegre, we visited the school, were very impressed, and immediately enrolled the boys to start classes in late February of 1970.

House hunting was not as easy. Jack Combs had diligently researched the rental market and took us to see several places. A few days later, we returned to Curitiba, empty-handed and discouraged. Porto Alegre was much bigger than Curitiba, and renting the kind of home we needed for the family and for the ministry was not going to be easy or cheap.

Time was running out when finally on January 19 we found a wonderful house. I wrote in a letter to friends,

> It's about a year old, lots of space for the family, big yard (with lots of flowers for Carol to dabble with), a telephone, which is like striking oil in the backyard . . . and an additional plus factor, the house is across the street from the school in which we enrolled the boys back in November! The boys are excited now more than ever about the move since they have seen the house and met some of the children in the neighborhood.

February 9 was moving day. It was also our son Daniel's eighth birthday. The boys have a special memory of standing in the empty kitchen eating birthday cake with the movers. It was the last thing Carol baked before her stove, still warm, was loaded on the truck.

Two days later we unloaded and moved into our new home, opening a new chapter in our lives. The boys looked forward to starting school and being able to sit around the breakfast table listening for the bell to ring in the school yard across the street. The neighborhood was a friendly place with a number of younger families just like ours. The family next door had five children, the oldest was eleven. If the crowd wasn't playing at our house, they were all playing next door. There was a neighborhood movie theater with special Saturday afternoon matinees that the boys loved to attend with their friends. For Kent, Daniel, and Brian, the move to Porto Alegre was a success from day one.

After the moving truck pulled away, we began the task of unpacking boxes and getting settled in our new home. We were racing against time; classes at the university began in just eighteen days. We also began making preparations for the invasion of the turma from Curitiba, planned for the weekend of March 20–22.

Repeating a pattern from Curitiba, Jack and I met at night to walk the streets and pray. Rua da Alfandega was a "people street" several blocks long through the heart of the downtown area. In the warm summer evenings it was jammed with people heading to theaters, coming out of restaurants, standing in front of coffee bars, or just grouped in circles carrying on conversations. It was a great place to pray.

The other thing Jack and I did in those first days of March was track down two students, Fernando Korndorfer and Robeto Blauth, who had come to faith as teenagers through the ministry of a Lutheran missionary and pastor, Jack Aamot. (Jim tells this story in *Living Proof*, published by NavPress in 1988.) Both Fernando and Roberto were eager to get involved in what we were doing, and they were key players from the start.

The big day finally arrived for the invasion that we had first talked about while sitting around that campfire in July of 1969. At noon on

Friday, March 20, eleven bleary-eyed people staggered off the bus after the thirteen-hour journey from Curitiba. I stuffed five of them in my little car and headed to a restaurant near the university. The rest of the group followed in Jack's car and a taxi. Roberto was waiting to welcome them at the restaurant and get them fed. After lunch they toured the campus and then hopped on a city bus to get to our home.

After supper, we spent the evening talking, playing cards, and listening to music. For our three boys it was like a homecoming, seeing friends from Curitiba that they had not seen in weeks. Between our place and the Combs' we managed to find a place for everyone to sleep—some in beds, others on foam pads on the floor. We regrouped the next morning. They divided up into two- and three-person teams and headed back to campus to contact students using a simple questionnaire.

This was one of the few times we used this kind of thing, simply because it didn't produce accurate results. What most frequently happened was that the student being interviewed responded with "correct" answers to such questions as "Who, in your opinion, was Jesus Christ?" The response was usually almost word for word what they had been taught in catechism. After several such responses, we would say, "Okay, those are nice answers. Why don't you tell me what you *really* think?" After a startled look, sometimes a sneer, we'd get answers like "He was just a great teacher" or "He was a revolutionary leader like Che Guevara."

The questionnaire did serve as an icebreaker to get a conversation started. The students from Curitiba would then explain that they were involved in small groups that met to read and discuss the life and teachings of Jesus, and that they were in town for the weekend to help start some similar groups in Porto Alegre. The conversation would include an invitation to a *churrasco* (a Brazilian-style barbecue) the next day to hear some of the results of the questionnaire.

On Sunday morning Jack and I, along with several of the Curitiba group, made runs downtown to bring people to our house. The living room was packed wall to wall with people who listened as Osvaldo described what was going on in Curitiba. He finished by saying that Ken and Jack were starting the same kind of thing here. Before the session ended, we set a date for our next gathering. We ended that weekend having established contact with about twelve students who were interested in continuing to meet with us.

Jack and I wrote a newsletter to friends back in the United States that month. It started out like this: "The question is not, 'Where are they?' In a city of over a million we are constantly surrounded by them. The question is, 'What can two of us do against a million?'" That weekend invasion was part of the answer. We just needed a little help from our friends.

We began with the students who jammed our living room that morning, and by the end of the year we had several small groups that were reading the Bible with us. Before the students left town in December, we had a special event to introduce my parents, Walt and Lucile Lottis, who had arrived to spend Christmas with us. My fondest memories of their visit were the times I sat with my dad and mom to translate as a student told the story of his or her personal journey to faith. My mom was particularly impressed with one such student, Vera Radünz.

We first met Vera through her brother, Egon, who was part of the initial group of students in Curitiba. She quickly fit into the turma in Porto Alegre during that year as she finished nurse's training. When she began to discuss with us the possibility of extending her studies for an additional year, we invited her to live in our home. Our three sons would agree that was one of the best decisions we ever made.

Vera was a delightful mix of Mary Poppins and Maria from *The Sound of Music*. Our boys were eleven, nine, and eight at that time. It became a Saturday morning routine for them to prepare a breakfast tray, knock on Vera's bedroom door, and then pile onto her bed to "help" her eat. She would in turn entertain them by playing the guitar and teaching them to sing Brazilian folk songs. To this day, the boys still consider Vera to be their *titia*, the affection word for "auntie."

Vera became a very special person in the life of our family as we shared our common citizenship in God's kingdom. We believe that the deep friendship we enjoy to this day was not just a consequence of that invasion of Porto Alegre but a fulfillment of Matthew 19:29: "And everyone who has left houses or brothers or sisters or father or mother or children or fields for my sake will receive a hundred times as much and will inherit eternal life."

Ken Lottis and Jack Combs sip cafezinho and study a map of Porto Alegre.

CHAPTER 13

CROSSING THE BRIDGE
IN FLORIANÓPOLIS

THE ISLAND OF Santa Catarina is nestled against the curve of the southern coastline of Brazil. Florianópolis, the capital city of the state of Santa Catarina, is located on the island, as is the Universidade Federal de Santa Catarina.

A narrow channel separates the island from the mainland and at its narrowest point is spanned by a beautiful but now aged suspension bridge. It is sort of a scaled-down version of San Francisco's Golden Gate Bridge. It was eventually replaced by a modern four-lane concrete structure and closed to vehicle traffic, but it remains a tourist attraction.

Carol and I, along with our three boys, crossed that suspension bridge early one summer morning in January of 1968. We were on our way to spend the day with Aldo and Aracy Berndt and their four-year-old son, Rogério. We had been vacationing together on the beach in Camboriú where Aldo and I had spent many hours getting better acquainted. That morning we were responding to their invitation to spend a day with them in Florianópolis.

Exactly one year before that, Aldo had sat on that same beach listening to Jim describe what we were doing in Curitiba. That conversation set off a chain of events in Aldo's life that were still in progress. We pulled up in front of Aldo and Aracy's home in our little blue Volkswagen, unaware that this visit would become one more event in the sequence.

A few minutes later we followed as Aldo led the way over winding cobblestone roads to the sparkling blue lagoon that was the center of the island's shrimp and seafood business. One side of the lagoon was lined with enormous dunes of powdery white sand. The four of us sat on the beach talking as we watched our four little boys dash back and forth between the water and the dunes. They would run up the side of a dune, sinking into the soft sand, then roll back down and scamper into the water, looking like sugared donuts.

After several hours of that, the boys were exhausted, and we were all ravenously hungry. We drove back around the edge of the lagoon and across a rickety wooden bridge to a seafood restaurant. It was a simple place—forget about air conditioning; instead, think several fans laboring to keep the hot, humid air moving.

Barefoot and still in our bathing suits, we were seated (the "no shoes, no shirt, no service" rule did not apply here) around a wooden table covered with a white plastic tablecloth. No knives or forks, just platters of shrimp. It was all-the-shrimp-you-can-eat, and we ate a bunch.

After the shrimp experience we returned to Aldo and Aracy's home, took showers, and while the boys played, we continued to talk. It was apparent that in one year's time, Aldo's activity as a Lutheran pastor had taken on a whole new direction. While carrying on his traditional duties, he was now discipling some of his parishioners, meeting with them one-on-one. He was also spending time at the campus, and his ministry was expanding among the students. Much of our conversation had to do with the growing tensions of juggling all these new activities.

Late that afternoon we drove back across that bridge, returning to Camboriú and the final days of our vacation. We left behind what amounted to a ticking time bomb that would eventually go off—two years later, as it turned out.

In early 1970, as we were getting settled in Porto Alegre and developing those initial contacts with students, Aldo was getting ready to cross a different kind of bridge.

He was in a very real sense a victim of his own success. His personal ministry in the lives of parishioners had grown beyond his ability to keep up. The work among students also had mushroomed. Something had to change. He called a meeting with his church board to convey his dilemma. In a letter, Jim related what Aldo had told them:

I explained what my pastoral activities required of me. Then I showed them what I had found to be my God-given calling. That is, discipling men who will lead out in the ministry. I expounded Ephesians 4:11-12. Then I showed them that I can hardly carry on this discipling ministry and carry the traditional responsibilities of the pastorate at the same time. For this reason I have been forced to make a decision, that is, that I cannot continue to work for them as their pastor and give myself to working with men—while they, with every right, expect something else of me (the fulfilling of the traditional functions).

In his letter, Jim then added, "This is sort of a devastating conclusion—and undoubtedly not valid in many situations, but I could say that Aldo is right in this case."

That ticking time bomb was no longer ticking. It hadn't exploded either. Instead it was being disarmed as Aldo began a strategic withdrawal from his role as a pastor with the Lutheran church.

Months later I received a telephone call from Aldo. He was taking an overnight bus from Florianópolis to Porto Alegre and wanted me to pick him up at the bus depot the next morning. After breakfast in our home I dropped him off at the Lutheran office where he initiated discussions that would eventually end his career as a pastor.

Back in Florianópolis he and Aracy crossed a bridge, figuratively and literally, when they left the parsonage next door to the Lutheran church and moved into their own home on the mainland to give themselves to the ministry of The Navigators in Brazil.

CHAPTER 14

WHAT HAPPENS AFTER GRADUATION?

GRADUATION FROM UNIVERSITY in Brazil is a big deal. The event itself is very formal and very long. The ceremony typically includes lengthy speeches from the class valedictorian, a university official, and a politician, or, as was frequently the case during the military dictatorship, some high-ranking officer from the Brazilian armed forces. These speeches were delivered in high oratorical fashion instead of the language of ordinary conversation, making them virtually impossible for us to understand. But they sure sounded impressive!

Being invited to a graduation was an honor. The invitation was hand-delivered, never sent by mail. It was elaborate and addressed with beautiful calligraphy. One of the first invitations we received, and certainly the most impressive, was from Evaristo Terezo, who graduated in December of 1967 with a degree in forestry management. The invitation was a hollow tube made of jacaranda wood with our names engraved in the finish. When opened, the tube held a rolled-up piece of parchment on which the details of the ceremony were written.

The month of December, like June in the Northern Hemisphere, is a time of graduations, dances, parties, and weddings. Christmas, at times, almost gets lost in the shuffle. During our first few years in Brazil, we attended many of these events. We felt honored to be a part of something normally reserved for family and very close friends.

But a troubling pattern began to emerge. Students who graduated and found jobs in the city where they were part of a turma did well in their spiritual development. Those who went back to their hometown, or to some distant location required by their employment, struggled. We began to spend more and more time in our team meetings discussing this, searching for solutions. I put in long days traveling to spend time with some of these people.

Dr. Paulo Sperka was an example. Paulo was a medical doctor, and when he graduated, the only place he could find work was in a small hospital in a farm town five hours driving time from Curitiba. About three of those hours were on dirt roads—hubcap-deep mud when it rained, clouds of dust when it didn't. One of three doctors, Paulo did a bit of everything: delivered babies, sewed up knife wounds, treated the common cold.

But Paulo and his wife, Lia, were lonely and spiritually isolated. On several occasions they traveled to Curitiba with their two small children to spend a weekend in our home and bathe in the warmth of their friends in the turma. As they would load up in their mud-spattered car to head home on a Sunday afternoon, I struggled with the question "How are we going to care for not just Paulo and Lia but hundreds of couples like this in the future?"

Within our organization, this was an unprecedented set of circumstances. Navigator student ministries in the United States, as well as in many other countries, had never faced this problem. There was a basic assumption that once they left university and entered the "real world," students would naturally find their way into an existing local church where they would have a context for ongoing outreach among their friends. That simply was not happening in Brazil. Years would pass before that assumption was examined and discarded in the United States and other countries. The reasons were not so much theological as they were cultural and social.

It was Aldo who brought biblical insight into our discussions of this issue. He systematically unpacked the New Testament history recorded in the books of Acts and Galatians of what happened when the gospel passed beyond the cultural walls of Judaism and penetrated non-Jewish nations.

The first crack in the wall appears in Acts 10 when Peter had a very disturbing vision that rattled his traditional Jewish doctrinal statement. While still trying to sort out what it all meant, he was summoned to visit Cornelius, a Roman centurion stationed in Caesarea. Confused, Peter stalled for time until the next day. He then formed a six-man committee to go along with him. My hunch is that as they traveled they spent the time talking and trying to figure out what was going on.

When they arrived at Cornelius's home, Peter was not exactly tactful as he explained the tradition prohibiting Jews from associating with Gentiles. Then apparently still unsure of himself he said, "May I ask why you sent for me?" (Acts 10:29).

He stumbled into his presentation, probably realizing his audience had little or no knowledge of Jewish history. Before he could finish his sermon, Cornelius's people began to respond and were filled with the Holy Spirit.

Dumbfounded, Peter turned to his committee with a question: "Can anyone keep these people from being baptized with water? They have received the Holy Spirit just as we have" (Acts 10:47).

That committee probably saved Peter's reputation because when they arrived back in Jerusalem, they were in deep trouble. The accusation: "You went into the house of uncircumcised men and ate with them" (Acts 11:3).

Fortunately Peter's story, backed up by those eye witnesses, was convincing: "When they heard this, they had no further objections and praised God, saying, 'So then, God has granted even the Gentiles repentance unto life'" (Acts 11:18).

In my imagination I picture those men walking out of that meeting, scratching their heads, mumbling in their beards, trying to figure out what just happened.

The next crack in the wall shows up in Acts 11:

> Those who had been scattered by the persecution in connection with Stephen traveled as far as Phoenicia, Cyprus and Antioch, telling the message only to Jews. Some of them . . . went to Antioch and began to speak to Greeks also, telling them the good news about the Lord Jesus . . . and a great number of people believed and turned to the Lord. (verses 19-21)

That crack also registered on the theological seismographs in Jerusalem. Greeks? Believing in our Jewish Jesus? How could that happen?

To check things out, they sent good old Barnabas. When he arrived, he saw that God was at work, encouraged them, and then did something that perhaps changed the course of what we now call church history. He went to Tarsus and recruited Paul to join him in Antioch. Acts 11:26 says they spent a year teaching great numbers of people. Interestingly, the disciples in Antioch were the first ones to be called followers of Christ (the Messiah), a designation apparently redundant for Jewish believers.

But as the message of Jesus spread among non-Jewish people, trouble was brewing in Jerusalem. Acts 15 tells the story. "Then some of the believers who belonged to the party of the Pharisees stood up and said, 'The Gentiles must be circumcised and required to obey the law of Moses'" (verse 5).

That became the issue for an historic meeting held in Jerusalem. At stake was the purity of the gospel as it crossed cultural lines. Peter became a major voice in the discussion because of his experience with Cornelius. Paul and Barnabas told story after story of the power of God being witnessed among the Gentiles. Then James put it all together in an incredible statement: "It is my judgment, therefore, that we should not make it difficult for the Gentiles who are turning to God" (Acts 15:19).

The two big things that were sure to "make it difficult" for the

Gentiles—circumcision and the Law of Moses—were off the table. Later Paul would pen these words: "For it is by grace you have been saved, through faith—and this not from yourselves, it is the gift of God—not by works, so that no one can boast" (Ephesians 2:8-9).

Our discussion of this subject with Aldo led us to Galatians 2:8-9:

> For God, who was at work in the ministry of Peter as an apostle to the Jews, was also at work in my ministry as an apostle to the Gentiles. James, Peter and John, those reputed to be pillars, gave me and Barnabas the right hand of fellowship when they recognized the grace given to me. They agreed that we should go to the Gentiles, and they to the Jews.

It became very clear to us that we had been given a ministry among "Gentiles," a generation of people who had abandoned the rigidity and the rites of their Catholic upbringing and were uncomfortable and often confused by the traditions and practices of evangelical Protestantism as it manifested itself in Brazil at that time. The gospel could continue to advance among these people if it remained unencumbered by what we referred to as "cultural barnacles."

While that clarified one issue, it raised a host of others. If those who came to faith in Christ through this ministry were not going to affiliate with existing churches, what implications did that have for the future? How were we going to provide for the long-term spiritual welfare of these people? That question became a major topic of discussion, study, and prayer in the early part of the 1970s.

A gathering in an open air café in a Curitiba park to celebrate the end of the school year. (*Left to right* Front: Osvaldo, Evaristo, Curt, Hans, Ken, Dinho, Paulo, Walter M., Egon, Onofre; Back: Walter J., Vanderlei, Renny, Sato, Nelson)

CHAPTER 15

WORKING OURSELVES OUT OF A JOB

JIM AND I had some disagreements. Nothing major. But there were some issues where we did not see eye to eye. For example, there were those desks in our little office in downtown Curitiba.

Jim had a brand-new executive-type desk, which he had purchased from some office supply store. It had a beautiful mahogany finish, nice tidy drawers, and a spotless sheet of plateglass on top.

I bought my desk from a used furniture place a few blocks from our office. It was a huge old-fashioned rolltop desk, covered in layers of dust and grime. I hired a couple of men and their horse-drawn cart to deliver it. It was so heavy that when they loaded it onto the cart, it lifted the horse slightly off the pavement and he was unable to gain traction!

I spent a day scrubbing it with soap and water, then rubbing it down with furniture polish. It had a wealth of drawers, slots, and pigeonholes and a variety of nicks, scars, and scratches from its years of use.

Once I settled in with my books and papers, the desktop was always cluttered. If a student arrived, I could hastily pull down the rolltop to conceal the mess.

When Jim saw that remarkable desk for the first time, he thought

I'd lost my mind. After a long discussion, he graciously allowed me to keep it but frequently made disparaging remarks about the "monster" after a late-night scare.

I had pulled down the rolltop when I left for the day but had failed to properly secure the latch. As Jim worked into the night, the latch gave way, and the rolltop slid out of its track and crashed to the floor a few feet from where he was sitting.

That put a strain on our relationship for a few days.

But there was one thing on which Jim and I shared identical convictions: our strong belief that we had to work ourselves out of a job. From the earliest stages of the work in Curitiba, we were turning over the leadership to the Brazilians.

When Jim and Marge left for a six-month visit to the United States, much of what he had been doing was handed off to men like Osvaldo and Mario. We did the same thing. No doubt in some instances the guys were not fully prepared to take the lead. But we felt that the message being conveyed was more important. And the message was that this was their deal, not ours.

When Carol and I moved to Porto Alegre, and a few months later Jim and Marge moved to Florianópolis, the ministry in Curitiba was left in the hands of the team led by Osvaldo Simões, which included Mario, Lenir, Fernando, and Walter.

An essential element in this process was to keep things simple. We watched other North American groups come into Brazil with huge quantities of money to set up their operations. They offered people jobs, salaries, and an identity. In so doing, the message conveyed was: "This is our deal; we own this. Maybe someday you'll be able to take over and run it."

Our setup, other than the homes we lived in, consisted of those two desks. That greatly simplified the process when Jim moved to Florianópolis for the purpose of preparing Aldo to lead the work in Brazil. There was no property to manage, no payroll to meet. Developing a deep friendship and a strong relationship was the top priority.

Jim and Aldo spent a lot of time on the road over the next eighteen months, tracking down students who had come to faith in Christ, had graduated, and were now scattered across a three-state area in southern Brazil. They logged more than 100,000 miles on Jim's car and were often away from home fifteen days a month.

What they found accentuated the need to devote time and creativity to helping these people. One fellow, six months into his career, had accumulated debt that exceeded what we would earn in the next five years. Another was facing criticism for the way he was managing a family-owned business; the problem was his attempts to be honest. They found couples were struggling with their marriage relationships due to the stress of long hours at work, pregnancies, and managing their finances. There was a single guy who took a teaching position in a small town a seven-hour drive from Curitiba. He quickly became the most eligible bachelor in town and fell in love with a local beauty. She began to question his involvement with the turma as religious fanaticism. Faced with the choice between his now-distant friends from his college days and this beautiful woman, he chose her.

Many of the students they visited had been in small-group Bible studies but had never started or led a group on their own. They needed help to simplify the process of getting into the Scriptures with new friends. As a result, during a team meeting in February of 1972, a decision was made that Carol and I would withdraw from the student ministry in Porto Alegre in June. We would spend a few months in the United States, and upon our return, we would initiate a ministry among the graduates.

In this case, I had not exactly worked myself out of a job. More accurately stated, the ministry among students had created a new job, one that would ultimately determine the long-term success or failure of this work in Brazil.

Neatly organized clutter in Ken's prized rolltop desk.

CHAPTER 16

CHANGING ROLES, CHANGING CITIES

"WHEN YOU STUDY the Bible with students in Brazil, do you use the King James Version?"

I stared in disbelief at the man asking the question. He was a middle-aged pastor who had recently taken over the small independent church in the town where Carol had grown up. The church, where Carol's mother still attended, had included us in their missions giving for nearly eight years. Now this man, a hard-core fundamentalist, seemed intent on changing that.

"The King James Version," I replied, stating what I thought was obvious, "is in English. The Bible we use is in Portuguese, which is the language of Brazil."

He pushed on. "Is the version that you use a translation of the King James into Portuguese?"

As I struggled to keep my composure, I realized I was fighting a battle I could not win. An hour and a half later I walked out into a warm Minnesota evening knowing we were about to lose the financial support from Carol's home church.

It was June of 1972, and we were beginning an eight-month visit in the United States. Spending time with donors and supporting churches was a necessity but also a challenge. While most people were excited to hear our stories, there were others, like this pastor, who seemed to focus on things that did not sound familiar or meet their traditional criteria.

The first stop on our itinerary was Minnesota to visit Carol's mother, her family, and our friends from our days at Northwestern College in the Twin Cities. But we appeared to be off to a bad start with that rather hostile interview, which left me weary and discouraged.

In stark contrast was the reception in Seattle a few days later. My brother Harold had introduced me to his pastor, Rev. Bud Palmberg, in January of 1969. It was one of those wonderful experiences where two people meet and immediate bonding takes place.

Now three years later, Bud warmly introduced me to his growing congregation at Mercer Island Covenant Church. The stories I told that Sunday morning were about what was happening in Brazil, and they were met with an enthusiastic response.

After church, the conversation continued over lunch at a nearby restaurant. As Bud listened to me describe in more detail what was happening with our students who graduated, his interest intensified. His attitude was one of affirmation rather than criticism. When I explained that I would be devoting three months in the fall to study in preparation for taking on my new assignment, he said, "Come by my office tomorrow. I have a book for you to read."

The next day I walked out of his office carrying a heavy, two-inch-thick copy of *By One Spirit* by Karl Olsson. It was a meticulously written history of what is now known as the Evangelical Covenant Church. It looked terribly boring, but I promised Bud I would read it. I didn't specify when. Somewhat like a dynamite charge with a long fuse, the content of that book would explode in my head a few months later.

We spent the rest of the summer visiting family and friends in Oregon and Washington. My parents were living on Thetis Island, British Columbia, which became home base for those weeks. My father had prepared all sorts of activities and adventures for Kent, Dan, and Brian, including a four-day cruise for our family through the Canadian

Gulf Islands on his twenty-four-foot boat. It was a wonderful summer with wonderful memories, a special gift, especially considering that it was my father's last summer on this earth.

In the second week of August we tried to figure out how to get our family, our luggage, and some newly acquired camping gear into the lovely 1967 two-door Mercury Cougar that my brother Loren and his wife, Marge, had given us. By strapping the spare tire on the lid of the trunk and shipping a couple of larger suitcases via Greyhound bus, we got along just fine!

When we arrived in Colorado Springs, the people at the headquarters of The Navigators helped us locate and rent a three-bedroom apartment and furniture and enroll the boys in a school a few blocks away. After months of travel, it was good to settle in our own place, even if we had to beg, borrow, or rent the furnishings we needed.

Not many people understand the emotional wear and tear that takes place in the lives of a missionary family during these traveling experiences. Our boys were cut off from their friends, constantly meeting new people, eating strange food, sleeping in different beds, and being asked dumb things like "Can you say something in Portuguese?" On one occasion, in a Sunday school class, Daniel was being taunted by an older boy. Using the training from his Brazilian judo instructor, he grabbed the boy, flipped him over his head, and slammed him to the floor. Not exactly the model of behavior expected from a missionary kid.

That rented apartment in Colorado Springs became a safe haven for the boys, as well as for Carol and me. Integrating into school brought a few surprises. A few weeks into the school year I wrote to a friend:

> The boys are doing well in school. Far better in fact than we anticipated. Brian is at the top of his class in reading, which is the biggest surprise. His teacher called a few weeks ago to ask us to help him understand the concept of vowels and consonants. . . . She said he seemed to know nothing about

them. When he arrived home, I asked him, "What are the *vogais*? Hearing the word in Portuguese, he immediately replied in Portuguese.

"So what are they in English?"

"I just told you." Then he smiled and said, "No, I said them in Portuguese, didn't I?"

So his whole problem was he did not understand the word *vowel*!

Once we were into a routine in our small apartment, I began looking for a place where I could study. I had hoped to find a niche at The Navigators office, but nothing turned up.

Then while having lunch with a longtime friend, Monte "Chuck" Unger, I learned he was running his freelance writing and photography business out of a suite of offices in downtown Colorado Springs—and he had office space he was using mostly for storage that I could move into. A few days later I was in business using an old door as a table, one of Chuck's typewriters, and a chair purchased at a furniture auction.

I will be forever indebted to Chuck for his hospitality, friendship, and the many hours of stimulating conversation we enjoyed. The days I spent in that office were not only personally restorative but allowed me the quiet hours I needed to study, pray, and think about what lay ahead.

The primary focus of that time was on what we were going to do to provide long-term care and leadership for those graduating from our student ministries. The same questions and issues continued to surface in the lives of these people.

High on the list of issues for our Brazilian friends were courtship and marriage. Raising children followed. Managing personal finances was a nightmare in Brazil's inflationary economy. Morality in the workplace was a minefield where bribery and under-the-table payoffs were a way of life. And how does this kingdom-of-God stuff we keep talking about make sense in everyday life?

When combined, these issues constituted something more than

just theory; it was all or nothing, do or die. Either we resolved this, or we looked for some other line of work. None of us wanted to continue to give ourselves to a ministry among students if, within two to five years after graduation, they were living as if the kingdom of God did not exist.

As I unpacked my books and papers on that door made into a desk, the big thick book that Bud Palmberg had loaned me stared up at me, waiting to be read. With reinforcement from Unger's coffeepot, I sat down one morning and began to read. Contrary to my initial impression, it was not boring. History, when properly written, should never be boring.

For the next few days I did little else but turn the pages of Olsson's story, which began in the early 1800s in a poverty-stricken, spiritually starved Sweden. What caught my attention early on was that God was at work, using minimal resources, to raise up a people for himself in Sweden. This took place within the shell of an institutional state church that had lost credibility to change people's lives. The generation of people who came out of that movement in Sweden had no vast organization to guide or sustain them. Rather they had learned from the very beginning to rely on the Scriptures, prayer, and mutual encouragement from the simple gatherings in their homes.

As I kept reading Olsson's story, I was constantly reminded that here was a story from church history where God stepped outside traditional boundaries and established patterns to raise up a new generation of his people. Then one afternoon I laid down Olsson's book and picked up my Bible. My imagination was captured by the imagery of these descriptive lines in Isaiah 49:8-12:

This is what the LORD says:

"In the time of my favor I will answer you,
    and in the day of salvation I will help you;
I will keep you and will make you

to be a covenant for the people,
to restore the land
and to reassign its desolate inheritances,
to say to the captives, 'Come out,'
and to those in darkness, 'Be free!'

"They will feed beside the roads
and find pasture on every barren hill.
They will neither hunger nor thirst,
nor will the desert heat or the sun beat upon them.
He who has compassion on them will guide them
and lead them beside springs of water.
I will turn all my mountains into roads,
and my highways will be raised up.
See, they will come from afar—
some from the north, some from the west,
some from the region of Aswan."

We were already seeing what the initial lines of this passage described. Captives, people in chains coming out of their spiritual darkness to be free. Now we were moving into the future where they would be fed and nourished "beside the roads" and "find pasture on every barren hill." A compassionate God would lead them to "springs of water" and turn all "mountains into roads."

When combined with Olsson's story, this passage gave me the assurance that God was at work, that he would care for us as we continued to use the keys to the kingdom that he had given us. Just as my friend had whispered to me in that airport, "One way or another, he'll get his church built."

*   *   *   *   *

After weeks of planning and preparation, on December 5, Aldo, his wife, Aracy, and their eight-year-old son, Rogério, walked off a plane in Colorado Springs. Aldo had come to participate in a leadership meeting and be introduced as Jim's successor in Brazil. His presence also opened a new chapter in my life as I began to build a relationship with this gifted man who was now the leader of The Navigators ministry in Brazil.

Two days after their arrival, leaving Rogério with Carol, Kent, Dan, and Brian, Aldo, Aracy, and I flew to California. We spent the next five days visiting campus ministries of The Navigators, with Dan Greene as our guide and chauffeur. When we returned to Colorado, we spent a day on the campus of the University of Colorado in Boulder and spoke to a Sunday morning Bible study for cadets at the U.S. Air Force Academy.

After the Christmas holidays, Carol and I and Aldo and Aracy attended a staff conference for The Navigators in Glorieta, New Mexico. During these days together, we laid the foundations for our relationship, both as friends and as colaborers in the ministry of The Navigators. In preparation for the trip, Aldo had worked at improving his English. Someone suggested he do some reading to build up his vocabulary and had loaned him several paperback westerns by Louis L'Amour. He quickly became a fan of L'Amour's stories and devoured book after book. It became a source of quiet amusement for me to sit in on one of Aldo's conversations in English and watch the faces of people when he interjected some of L'Amour's cowboy vocabulary, such as "that saved my bacon," into a sentence.

I added to that western mystique by often introducing myself and Aldo as the Brazilian version of Butch Cassidy and the Sundance Kid.

, , , , ,

A few days after staff conference, our two families boarded a flight from Colorado Springs to Miami, where we would connect to a flight to Brazil. We hit some extremely rough air, and by the time we arrived in Miami, Aracy was violently ill, unable to do any more traveling. With only a brief layover, Aldo and I had to come up with a solution.

We canceled their reservations for that evening's flight, and they were put on a standby list for the next few nights. Between the two of us, we had very little cash. We went into the lobby of the hotel that operated inside the Miami airport to ask for a room. Fortunately they had a vacancy. I explained our situation to the manager, and he made an imprint of my American Express card. I signed the blank voucher, and Aldo took the key and put Aracy to bed.

Aldo, Rogério, and I did a quick tour of the airport so that I could show them where to get food, using what cash we had between us. Then, racing to the departure gate, I joined my family to board the flight home.

A few nights later, space opened up on a flight to Brazil. Aldo checked Aracy out of the hotel, picked up a rather healthy bill on my American Express card, and began their journey home.

The Miami International Airport is part of a very special set of memories for this Butch Cassidy and his friend, the Sundance Kid. It gave us a great story of how we "saved his bacon." In the years that followed, this became something of a blueprint for our relationship as we teamed up to work together.

Arriving back in Brazil, both Aldo and I set about to move our families to Curitiba. Now it was time to settle in the same city and get to work.

CHAPTER 17

CAMELS, HORSES, AND BIG SUNDAYS

THE HOUSE WE rented in February of 1973 had the appearance of a fortress. Located on a corner lot in one of Curitiba's older neighborhoods, the house and yard were about fifteen feet above street level. Surrounded by a stone wall and a Laurel hedge, it seemed impregnable. In reality it was part of a traffic pattern for burglars who roamed the neighborhood. I eventually lost track of all the stuff that got carried off by late-night "visitors." On one occasion I awoke during the night to the sound of a window rattling. I opened the door to the guest bedroom, switched on the light, and found myself staring at a burglar perched on a ladder outside the window, trying to force it open.

The house itself, however, was ideal for what we would be doing for the next few years. There were five bedrooms, two of which were upstairs and the boys excitedly claimed as theirs. Rather than share space with one of his brothers, Brian opted for a large attic closet that he transformed into a bedroom. Thus, we were able to have overnight guests downstairs without disturbing the boys. There was a drawback: the house had only one bathroom! The large backyard had a few fruit trees and a fenced-in pen where Dan raised a few chickens. At the back of the lot was a covered barbecue and picnic area that we immediately put to use.

Moving back to Curitiba was simplified by the fact that we were familiar with the city. The boys returned to the school they had previously attended. Kent and Daniel attended class in the morning, catching a bus across the street from the house. Brian boarded a Volkswagen van that picked him up outside our front gate.

Carol was delighted to discover that on Monday mornings a farmer's market was set up on the street beside our house. We had fresh fruit and vegetables literally at our front gate. A block away, a small bakery and a butcher shortened our supply lines for bread, milk, and meat.

These were important details as the volume of traffic through our home rose sharply in the next few months. There was a stretch during which we had overnight guests twenty-five out of forty nights. On more than one occasion we would make a hurried trip up the street to buy more bread, cold cuts, and cheese to feed unexpected guests.

As the family was settling into a routine, I began circulating among the university students who were involved in the ministry, which was now led by Mario and Sueli Nitsche. Of particular interest to me were those students who were beginning their final years and would be graduating in December of 1973 and 1974. I began attending a weekly Bible study that met in Mario and Sueli's apartment; it gave me the opportunity to meet and get acquainted with an impressive number of students who were all new believers.

At the same time I also began to track down former students who had found employment and stayed in Curitiba. Several were either dating or engaged, and there were a few newlywed couples. Carol and I began to host a weekly Bible study in our home for these folks. After years of leading studies with single students, it was a new experience to have couples romantically snuggling together on our couch. They often seemed more intent on holding hands than holding their Bibles and paid more attention to one another than to the discussion.

I also began to do some traveling to establish contact with those who had graduated and returned to their hometowns or moved to some distant city where they found employment.

Nelson and Gita had settled in their hometown of Joinville after some postgraduate study in Germany. I began to make the grueling two-hour drive once a week to help them start a Bible study group in their apartment. After we would finish at ten or ten thirty, I'd swallow one more shot of black coffee and start the drive home. The highway wound its way up through the coastal mountains, and at night the mixture of rain, fog, and long lines of trucks made it a nerve-racking trip.

The other priority during those initial months was to build a working relationship with Aldo. He was still living in Florianópolis and would stay there until June when Jim and his family moved to Colorado Springs.

His first visit to Curitiba that year was for the purpose of enrolling his son, Rogério, in school, and looking at a few apartments. We spent the day together and had pulled into my driveway in the midst of an intense conversation. I had learned by that time that most of my conversations with Aldo were intense, but always very stimulating. He possessed an ability to cut through all that was superfluous and zero in on the essential. That's exactly what he did as we sat in my car as darkness descended.

Pointing his finger in my face, he asked, "I want to know why I was chosen to take Jim's job rather than you. Do you feel that you should be the one to take over rather than me? Did anyone ask you about this?"

I had to admit that I had not been asked. Then I added, "If I had been asked, my answer would have been that I think my job should be to stay behind when Jim leaves and do all I can to help Aldo be successful. Rather than be known as the guy who took over when Petersen pulled out, I would prefer to be known as the guy who helped you make the Brazil ministry a Brazilian ministry."

I then drew on Aldo's familiarity with the Far West and compared myself to the man who "rode shotgun" on a stagecoach. "You drive the stagecoach; I'll ride shotgun and do my best to protect your back and keep the bad guys away."

We both laughed, but that metaphor did define one of my roles in a working relationship with Aldo in the years ahead. The bad guys in this situation were not really bad guys. In most cases they were just well-intentioned people in our Colorado Springs office who would contact Aldo with some irrelevant administrative question. Like the memo he received asking for his opinion on a proposed change to a new corporate logo for The Navigators. Rolling his eyes, he handed it to me, saying, "Take care of this!"

In those initial weeks, Carol and I began to talk about what we were sensing in regard to the people we had known as students who were now working professionals. There were some fundamental needs that they all had in common. One such issue was time management. As students, they had a lot of discretionary time that made it relatively easy to meet for Bible study, go to a movie with a friend, or get into a pickup game of soccer over a weekend.

Now as working professionals, free time was at a premium. Showing up on time for a weeknight study group was often in conflict with demands at work or traffic jams on the way home. Hanging out until after midnight to chat with friends made for a sluggish start at work the next morning. Weekends were prime time for shopping, running errands, and normal social activities.

In big cities like Rio de Janeiro and São Paulo, it could take several hours to drive across town to participate in a Bible study or just have dinner with friends. All of this brought additional stress to already busy lives, especially to newly married couples.

In response to what we were seeing, Carol and I put together an idea for a once-a-month, all-day gathering on Sunday we called a *Domingão* (Big Sunday). The core concept came from what I had learned while growing up in Oregon and from reading history about circuit-riding preachers. On horseback, these courageous clergymen would establish a circuit among the homesteaders and settlers scattered across a wide area. Upon the circuit rider's arrival in one of the locations, entire families would come in horse-drawn wagons and buggies from miles around. A time of worship and teaching would be followed by a picnic, games, and visiting. Before leaving, a date would be set for their next gathering, often weeks away.

Carol came up with the phrase that people needed to learn to "drink like camels instead of like horses."

With those foundational ideas we put together the plan for our first Domingão. We started at nine in the morning with coffee, fresh pãoz-inho, and an assortment of cheeses and cold cuts. At ten we gathered for a time of Bible study that focused on a specific topic or question. After about an hour, we divided into small groups to discuss how what we were learning from Scripture related to our everyday lives.

At noon we stopped for lunch. Carol had mastered the culinary skills to prepare a tasty meal for a lot of people on a limited budget. Lunch was followed by free time when people could play chess, listen to music, start a card game, watch a Formula One race on television, or just chat. Around three we served a round of cafezinho and gathered to share stories about what was going on in our lives. We ended the afternoon in a time of prayer.

The first Domingão was enthusiastically received, and we set a date, four weeks away, for our next gathering. Word of mouth promoted the idea, and more people showed up than we expected. We were off and running with a simple ministry model to meet the needs of graduating students as well as those already out of school.

We also observed that there were often individual issues stemming from a person's past. Creating a safe place to deal with these things had to be part of what we were doing. Often at the end of a Domingão, as students were saying their good-byes, someone would pull me or Carol aside and say, "There's some stuff that I need to talk to you about" or "My boyfriend and I would like to talk with you and your husband sometime."

On an evening when a young couple would come to our home, we sometimes served an early supper to the boys and got them settled for the night. Carol would set the table with a linen tablecloth and napkins, her fancy china, and candles. The meal would be simple, often a hearty homemade soup, accompanied with thick slices of whole wheat bread, cheese, and a glass of wine. All of that helped to create an atmosphere that was warm, intimate, and safe.

It became clear to us that for most of these young people, this was the first opportunity they had ever had to unpack some of the heavy burdens they were carrying. They came with questions about courtship and engagement, premarital sex, conflicts with their parents, and financial problems. Other concerns included issues of guilt, a troubled conscience, sexual or physical abuse, inappropriate behavior, and in some cases just curiosity about how, as Christ followers, we related to one another as husband and wife.

I will never forget one such conversation with a newly married couple. Before launching into a virtual laundry list of questions about marriage and raising children, they remarked, "You and Carol are the only couple we know who have been married for more than just a few years, have school-age children, and are followers of Christ. You're the only ones we can talk to about these things."

Those words echoed through my head for weeks as I pondered the unique set of circumstances in which we were living. Here we were in a city of nearly one million inhabitants, in one of the largest nations in the world, and we were the only couple they knew.

We were surrounded by a new generation of believers who had made serious commitments to follow Christ, obey his Word, and share what they were learning with others. As they grew in their awareness of all that commitment involved, we were their primary resource. They did not have the option of turning on a radio and listening to a psychologist with a God-centered worldview talk about marriage and family. Most of the books sold in Christian bookstores at that time were of little help. They had been written by authors who knew little or nothing about the Brazilian culture. When translated from English into Portuguese, they were laced with evangelical jargon, having been written for North American readers.

During this period, Carol and I would frequently talk about the extraordinary opportunity God had given us. At the same time, it was humbling, almost frightening, as we realized the implications of what we were doing. Like pioneers, we were blazing a trail through unmapped territory that the next generations would follow. Prayer for wisdom and guidance was a top priority.

In the midst of all this activity, I was living under a dark cloud of personal sorrow. My father had been diagnosed with a terminal malignant brain tumor. One day in June, Mario Nitsche showed up unexpectedly at our home to tell me he had received a call from my family. I followed him back across town to his apartment and placed a call to my brother Loren. My father had died in a small hospital in Chemainus, British Columbia. He was seventy-three. I am seventy-three as I write this.

Dr. Mario Nitsche makes a presentation during a weekend seminar.

CHAPTER 18

SURVIVING IN THE JUNGLE OF THE FIFTH LARGEST CITY IN THE WORLD

WHEN OSVALDO SIMÕES passed the entrance exams and entered the Universidade Federal do Paraná to major in chemical engineering, he was the essence of what Jesus described in Matthew 13:37 as "good seed."

By the time he graduated in December of 1972, he left a vibrant group of new believers roaming the halls of his alma mater. It was yet another example of how the good news of the kingdom flows through natural relationships in the Brazilian culture.

It came as no surprise at those first Domingóes that there were a lot of chemical engineers showing up. One of these, Evilásio Gioppo, caught my attention. Not only had he influenced many of his friends in engineering school, his entire family had been affected. His sister, Maria Lúcia, and her boyfriend, Alcides Ferré, were involved in the Bible study group and participated in the Domingóes.

As I got better acquainted with Evilásio, the subject of São Paulo was a frequent topic of conversation. For graduating chemical engineers, São Paulo was the major job market in the country. At the same time, the sheer size of the city was intimidating. For students like Evilásio, who had grown up in a small town, the traffic, the noise, the pollution, and the pace of life in São Paulo were menacing if not flatout terrifying.

My familiarity with São Paulo was very limited. On my first attempt to drive across the city, I became hopelessly lost. I didn't have a clue as to where I was. Pulling over to the curb, I asked a taxi driver for directions, but his answer was so long and convoluted that I asked if he would just lead the way and let me follow. It was a crazy few minutes as I tried to keep up with him. He knew that he wasn't going to get paid if he lost me. Eventually he pulled up to the curb, pointed to the next stoplight, and said, "Take a right at the light, and you're on the highway to Curitiba." I gratefully paid the fare and profusely thanked him for his help.

One of the last times I drove in São Paulo, I had gotten tangled up in the evening rush-hour traffic on a three-lane boulevard that abruptly became a two-lane street. I got pinched between two trucks, simultaneously crunching both front and back fenders. So it was with much apprehension that Evilásio and I mapped out a plan for winter break in July of 1973.

Industries in Brazil frequently accept university students for shortterm internships, called *estágios*. Whether paid or unpaid, these internships proved to be invaluable experience when applying for a full-time position.

Our plan was to load three or four of Evilásio's friends into my Volkswagen Variant and spend a week in São Paulo searching for estágios.

The key to our São Paulo plan was Renny Schmidt. Renny and Osvaldo had worked together in a small chemical plant in Curitiba in the early 1960s. As Osvaldo began to read the Bible with Jim, he shared with Renny what he was learning. Curious, Renny joined the sessions, and within a year Osvaldo and Renny were cocitizens of God's kingdom.

Of all the people with whom I became acquainted during my years in Brazil, Renny Schmidt stands out as one of the most extraordinary. Born into a humble rural family, he made his way to Curitiba, found employment, put himself through school, and was newly married to Arlene when I first met him in 1965.

While he was working in the laboratory with Osvaldo, he attended night school to obtain technical certification as a chemist. Gifted with a brilliant mind, he quickly attracted the attention of management with his skill in handling the manufacturing of industrial resins. On numerous occasions the company would rush him to the Curitiba airport and put him on a plane to São Paulo to troubleshoot a problem in their resin production plant there.

When he completed night school, an Italian company signed him to a lucrative profit-sharing agreement and moved him to São Paulo. After hearing the idea that Evilásio and I were working on, he eagerly agreed to host us in his home and help us find our way around the city.

On a chilly July evening a few weeks later, Evilásio and I, along with three other students, stood around Renny's outdoor barbecue pit, nibbling freshly grilled sausage and talking about life in São Paulo. The next morning we threaded our way through rush-hour traffic to Renny's plant.

As we walked alongside those huge reactors that stood three stories tall and around the maze of pipes and tubes, Renny explained the complexity of his job. It required a delicate balance of chemical reaction, extreme temperature, and high pressure over an extended period of time. "Do you know what happens if something goes wrong inside that reactor?" He paused, waiting for an answer.

One of the students spoke up. "Yes. During a demonstration in the lab at the university, the professor overheated the mixture and it turned solid. It was like glass. He had to throw the experiment into the trash."

"Exactly," Renny snapped. "That's the difference between a lab at school and this place. If that mixture turns solid, we have to shut down production, take the reactor apart, put a crew inside with jackhammers to clean it out. The company loses a lot of money, and I probably lose my job."

As he finished speaking, I quickly glanced at Evilásio and his friends. They were wide eyed in awe. This was the real world of a chemical industry.

Over the next few days, following Renny's suggestions and instructions, I drove nearly 350 miles around the city of São Paulo to visit the gigantic industrial complexes of companies like Mercedes-Benz, Volkswagen, Anderson-Clayton, and other multinational companies. At each location I would pull up to the front gate, say a quick prayer, drop off the students, find a place to park, and wait while they sought information on internship openings for January and July of 1974.

In some places they never made it past the front gate. In others they would be gone for more than an hour, returning elated with the way they had been received and what they had learned.

I arrived home at the end of that week, exhausted from the long hours behind the wheel but very satisfied with what we had accomplished. I was caught by surprise, however, as I picked up on the repercussions from students to what we had done. I had often taught that the kingdom of God penetrates all areas of life. But when I spent a week chauffeuring four students around São Paulo to look for internships, that message was conveyed in a new and dramatic fashion.

At the Domingão in August an engaged couple approached me with a question: "We feel we need to talk to someone about our upcoming marriage. But we weren't sure you would have time for that kind of thing until you made that trip to São Paulo. Could we get together with you and Carol sometime, just to talk?"

The other consequence of that trip was that Evilásio began to share with me his ideas for moving to São Paulo after graduation in December of 1974. He wanted to form a team that would begin looking for jobs and housing but would limit their search to a specific area of the city.

This would allow them to stay in touch during the week, get together socially, and meet for Bible study and prayer.

Evilásio's initiative was gaining momentum when I received a letter from a physics professor at Utah State University, Dr. Vern Peterson. He was looking at a job offer from the Institute of Astronomy and Geophysics at the University of São Paulo. Married with three children, he wanted to know how, if he took the job in São Paulo, they might tie in with what we were doing there.

We had, in fact, been looking for someone like Vern, a working professional rather than someone supported by donors who, with a family, could establish a home base for the work in São Paulo.

I wrote in response,

If you like clean air, disciplined traffic, and a relaxed suburban lifestyle, São Paulo is a wipeout. If, however, you could get excited about being a part of one of the world's noisiest and fastest growing cities, living in air polluted by some of the world's major industries, and driving in some of the world's most colossal traffic congestion, you'll love São Paulo.

Undeterred by that description and with a strong sense of God's leading, Vern and his wife, Bobbe, moved ahead with their plans. He accepted the job at the University of São Paulo, and they arrived at the end of June in 1974.

We spent the first few days together in a hotel in São Paulo. That gave us an opportunity to get acquainted with each other and them to meet Renny and his family. They began looking for housing, and, with some assistance from the university, were soon settled in a place in the same part of the city where Evilásio and his friends would be looking for jobs.

Vern and Bobbe had lived in Peru for three years while he worked as an atmospheric research physicist. Initially, they were somewhat limited as they "converted" their Spanish over to Portuguese. But they were a mature couple with cross-cultural experience, gifted in the area of hospitality, and they made an invaluable contribution in the months and years ahead.

The school year ended in December with graduation celebrations. Early in January, Evilásio and three other newly graduated chemical engineers—Aloir, Julio, and Cesario—traveled to São Paulo not just to look for jobs but to establish themselves as a turma, a community of followers of Jesus Christ.

They pooled their savings, rented a small house, and began pounding the pavement. By word of mouth the news circulated through the turmas in Rio, Florianópolis, Porto Alegre, and Ribeirão Preto, and in a spontaneous fashion people began to pray for the "São Paulo pioneers." Some groups collected money and sent it to help pay the rent and buy groceries.

Aloir was the first to land a job after Renny successfully created a position in his factory for an additional engineer. Aloir's first paycheck ceremoniously went into their common account and covered the cost of a party to celebrate. But Aloir had a higher priority for his next paycheck. He and his fiancée, Teresinha, had set a wedding date for July. Finding and furnishing an apartment became his focus.

One by one the others landed jobs, Evilásio being the last one, after nearly a year of applications, interviews, and waiting.

Throughout that year, I was making trips to São Paulo every three to four weeks. I would take an overnight "sleeper" bus, equipped with comfortable recliner seats, leaving Curitiba at eleven Friday night and arriving in São Paulo at five thirty or six the next morning. I would grab one of the ubiquitous Volkswagen Bug taxis and show up at the guys' house for breakfast.

Most mornings that meant pounding on the door to wake someone up and then walking down the street to buy bread and milk while they made coffee. On some occasions I would go to Vern and Bobbe's house, which I secretly preferred, knowing that Bobbe would be up and have coffee waiting when I arrived.

Those weekends included a Domingão-type gathering at Vern and Bobbe's or at Renny and Arlene's. In a letter written in June of that year I described it this way:

> The city of São Paulo has nearly eight million inhabitants. That's about twice the population of Norway. We decided sometime back that the first step to begin a Navigator ministry in such a city would be to have a team go in to establish a beachhead. These people and their children are that team . . . on the beach!

This team began to creatively respond to the challenge of living in this huge metropolis. They learned how to use the gigantic restaurants that dotted the distant suburbs and countryside around São Paulo. These "destination" establishments were family oriented and typically included a playground, a wading pool, a petting zoo, amusement park rides for children, and, of course, a family-style dining area. Capable of seating hundreds of patrons at a time, these locations could handle a group of twenty-five or fifty people on Saturday or Sunday.

The group from São Paulo would agree during the week to arrive at a designated location on a Saturday or Sunday morning. They would reserve tables for the entire group and turn the children loose to run and play. These environments were a refreshing break from the pollution and pressure of the city.

While the children played, the adults could sip cafezinho, nibble appetizers, enjoy a leisurely meal, and carry on nonstop conversations. This was an existing cultural model in São Paulo that the group adapted to their needs to stay in touch, spend time in prayer together, and allow their children to develop relationships.

The São Paulo people also perfected the art of weekend getaways. Within a ninety-minute drive, there were numerous European-style spa resort hotels. There were also a variety of retreat centers run by different Catholic orders, such as the Benedictines.

Every three to four months, the group from São Paulo would leave town after work on Friday and congregate at one of these locations. Carol and I were invited to participate in some of these gatherings. We would spend a few hours on Saturday morning digging into the Scriptures on a given topic, such as husband/wife relationships. The afternoon would be free for rest, recreation, and play time with the children. After dinner could be another discussion or a party time with games or dancing. Sunday mornings provided one more time for gathering around the Scriptures and extended prayer.

This type of weekend activity was a variation of the Domingão that originated in Curitiba. It allowed people in the turma to grow in their faith and develop strong bonds of friendship between families. But equally important was the fact that it left other weekends available for spending time with neighbors and friends from work. This was of vital importance for developing the relational networks through which the gospel could flow naturally. Spiritual survival in São Paulo was built around this kind of lifestyle, which employed social forms and structures that were indigenous to a great city.

Renny Schmidt gives his version of The Navigators "hand" illustration to a group of students.

CHAPTER 19

BUILDING MARRIAGES, RAISING CHILDREN, AND MOVING TO MINOT

IN THE MONTHS preceding our move to Brazil, Carol and I visited friends in Minot, North Dakota. Its remote location eventually evolved into an expression that we used as a form of code language. "Moving to Minot" blended irony and humor to communicate that we were discouraged, ready to pack up and leave Brazil. Somehow Minot (with my apologies to any readers who live there) became a destination to which we could escape into anonymity and no one would ever find us. Sort of a witness protection program for exhausted and failed missionaries.

I would come home after a bad day, walk up to Carol, and say, "Let's move to Minot." She would immediately understand, respond with a sympathetic smile, and wait to hear about my disastrous day. Or I would walk in to find that the washing machine had broken down again, the water system was shut off for repairs, and our three boys had declared civil war against each other. Carol's grim-faced greeting would be, "How soon can we leave for Minot?"

On more than one occasion, Minot was used at the end of an argument or a tense situation in our marriage. And there were plenty of those. Surrounded by people who were fifteen to twenty years younger than us, we suffered from the lack of peer relationships. Trying to maintain a healthy marriage under those circumstances was at times like navigating with radar that produced nothing more than a black screen.

In an effort to break the often icy silence after a marital storm, we would hold each other in an embrace, and one of us would say, "Should we just pack up and move to Minot tomorrow?"

Perhaps as a result of the effort required to maintain our marriage, we felt we had been uniquely prepared to help young Brazilian couples. We were in many cases the only example they had ever seen of a biblically based marriage.

During the early years of our marriage, we were profoundly helped by Dr. Henry Brandt, a Christian psychologist, author, and speaker. Listening to Henry's public teaching laid some foundational principles that we have built upon. Personal conversations in our home, along with his books, provided additional insight into things we needed to work on. Then in the fall of 1968 during our visit in the United States, I spent two weeks working alongside Henry, sitting in on his counseling sessions, listening to him speak, and bombarding him with questions. All of that background came together as a resource for the hours we were investing in these young couples.

It was only natural that in Brazil, the world's most populous Catholic nation, the institution of marriage as a cultural form was dominated by the church. On busy Saturdays, a local parish church would have weddings scheduled back-to-back from early morning into the evening hours. In most cases the bride and groom had selected that particular church based on its location, architecture, availability, or cost. Rarely was there any relationship between the couple and the priest who performed the ceremony. The result was an assembly-line process that was very impersonal.

At one such wedding, I watched as the priest invited the bride and groom to approach the altar. He began with the typical, "Brothers and sisters, we are gathered here today, in the presence of God, to witness the marriage of . . ." At that point he paused, looked at his watch, then consulted a slip of paper. Finding the names of the two people to be married at that hour, he went on, ". . . to witness the marriage of Maria and Pedro." The poor guy had no idea who he was about to unite in the bonds of holy matrimony.

On more than one occasion Carol and I entered a church to discover a ceremony already in progress. We were not late; they were! Inevitably by midafternoon, the traffic congestion of wedding guests, photographers, limousines, and newlyweds could get confusing, even humorous. Some friends of ours arrived late at a wedding and slipped into an empty pew at the back of the church. It was not until the ceremony ended and the newlyweds, two people they had never seen before, made their way up the aisle that they realized their mistake. The wedding they were to attend was running more than an hour behind schedule.

While the Catholic Church controls the cultural institution of marriage, for the vast percentage of the population, that control does not translate into adherence to the church's teachings. Prohibitions regarding the use of contraceptives, for example, fell into total disregard following the arrival of the pill in Brazilian pharmacies. In 1977, the Brazilian government chose to ignore pressure from the Vatican and the bishops of Brazil to pass its first divorce law.

So it was no surprise that the subject of fidelity in marriage as taught by the church had virtually no credibility. The sexual revolution that swept through the United States in the 1960s was merely an echo of what had seemingly characterized Brazilian behavior for decades. In a word, promiscuity was the accepted norm. This, then, was the stage upon which we would respond to questions and teach about marriage for the next few years.

Initially there was the tendency to reject our lifestyle as a model with the explanation that it was North American. We knew that wasn't true. But rather than argue that point, we simply turned to the Bible. These people had come to faith in Christ as a result of drawing conclusions from their own investigations of the Bible. The authority of the Scriptures, therefore, had already been established in their lives.

Beginning with conversations over dinner or around the coffee table in our living room, we began responding to questions by turning to passages of Scripture. Then in small group discussions we assembled the essential components of biblical teaching on marriage.

To facilitate the communication of this material, I began experimenting with a simple sketch of a house that was constructed on a foundation that was identified as the person of Christ. On that foundation I laid the floor of forgiveness. The exterior walls that I outlined were love and communication, with the roof providing the protection and security that come from the act of marriage. Finally an interior wall was added to the design to portray the intimacy of the sexual aspects of the relationship. I have no idea how many times during those years Carol and I used that material, continuing to add new anecdotes and experiences to keep it fresh.

Following on the heels of this subject were questions about raising children. Everyone seemed to be an expert on this subject until they became parents. One father commented, "Our little boy arrived, seemingly programmed to behave, and never gave us any problems. We thought raising children was easy. Then we had our little girl."

One of the things we observed during our initial years in Brazil was a general permissiveness in regard to children's behavior. Especially little boys. As our boys would invite friends over to play, we noticed that they seemed oblivious to anything we had to say. They would appear almost startled when our boys would respond to instructions or requests.

The pattern that most frequently surfaced was that parents assumed if they talked enough, repeated a phrase over and over, eventually their child would understand and behave in an appropriate way.

It became a common occurrence to visit a home and observe that dad and mom had completely lost control. They were being terrorized by their two-year-old. We watched this play out one day as a toddler went around the living room, pulling books off a shelf, then dragging pillows from the sofa across the floor. He seemed intent on doing anything to interrupt our conversation and, of course, to draw attention to himself. Repeated pleas to "stop that" or "don't touch those things" went unheeded. Finally he approached the dining room table and grabbed the lace tablecloth. Urgent appeals were made to "let go of the tablecloth" and "move away from the table." Staring defiantly, and with what seemed like an attempt to emulate a popular parlor trick, he jerked the tablecloth, toppling a crystal vase full of flowers onto the floor.

The stunned parents threw their hands in the air and almost in chorus said the same thing: "What are we going to do with this boy?" After helping clean up the mess, we began to offer some suggestions. But once again we sensed resistance, that these were part of our North American orientation to life and raising children.

We went to the Scriptures and, as we had done before, began to explore the biblical principles that are timeless and transcend culture. As we met with individual couples, we began to develop a list of their basic questions and the challenges they faced with their children. We could then match those issues to the resources available in the Bible.

At some point in this process I recalled hearing our friend Dr. Brandt explain why he left his clinical practice to spend more time speaking to groups of people. He realized that many of the problems he dealt with in his counseling practice could have been treated or even avoided had those people been exposed to some simple teaching.

Carol and I reflected on this as we were celebrating our wedding anniversary in the beach town of Camboriú. We were staying in a small, family-run hotel a half block from the beach. We began to talk about the possibility of a weekend retreat for couples in a hotel like this. It would be something of a precedent-setting event if we could pull it off.

We approached the owner of the hotel with our idea and discussed rates and prices. They had never hosted a group that filled their entire hotel but were eager to do whatever was needed to make the weekend a success.

The plan was to begin with a Friday evening meeting, have sessions Saturday morning and evening, and close with a final session Sunday morning. Even with deeply discounted rates from the hotel owners, it was going to be expensive for many of the young couples.

It was a tough sell. It meant asking time off work on a Friday afternoon. Driving time required as much as five hours on the road. In several cases I told couples who were in doubt about spending that much money, "If at lunch on Sunday you feel like it was not worth it, I'll give you a full refund. No questions asked."

The meeting room in the hotel that Friday night was filled. We had sixty-eight people in the hotel and fifteen more staying in private beach houses nearby. I don't remember what I talked about that evening, but it was obvious we were touching open nerves.

People were in tears as the meeting ended. One couple stayed up most of the night in a loud argument that kept people in the next room awake. As I circulated around the tables at lunch on Sunday, nobody asked for their money back.

Over the next few years we had other similar weekend events with the same objective. It was clear that a new generation of families was being formed. One of those new families was Dalby, whom you met in chapter 11, and his new bride, Jane, who were married in December of 1974.

During those months in 1969 that Dalby and I were reading through the gospel of John, he was making weekend trips to his hometown with the charming name of Pato Branco (White Duck). On Saturday evenings he would gather some of his friends and lead them in a discussion of the same chapter in John we had just finished. One of the participants in those discussions was a tall, bright-eyed high school girl name Jane. Now five years later, Jane was a devoted follower of Christ and Dalby's wife.

Another curious observer of those Saturday night discussions in

Pato Branco was a young priest, Valter. After a conversation with Dalby that extended into the early-morning hours, Valter shook his head. "You really believe this stuff, don't you?"

"Don't you?" was Dalby's startled response.

"I wish I did."

A few years later Valter was transferred to a downtown parish in Curitiba, where Dalby introduced us a few months prior to his wedding. Out of respect for Jane's family, they were to be married in a Catholic church, and Valter had agreed to conduct the ceremony. But there was one complication.

Dalby had asked Carol and me to be his godparents, which was a real honor. But he wanted me to bring the homily during the ceremony instead of Valter. This was not standard protocol, and I expected a polite but firm refusal. To my surprise, Valter agreed and thought it was a wonderful idea.

Thus a few weeks later Carol and I walked into one of the oldest churches in Curitiba to participate in Dalby and Jane's wedding. The church was packed with family, friends from the turma, and business colleagues from the architectural firm where Dalby worked. I was probably more nervous than the groom.

Valter worked his way through the legal and religious preliminaries and then gave me a nod. Carol and I were standing to the right of Dalby and Jane, so both couples turned slightly to face each other. My knees were shaking. This was the largest crowd I had ever spoken to during my years in Brazil.

As I began my talk, I was aware of a sudden hush in the audience. Normally in a Brazilian wedding nobody pays much attention to what the priest has to say. But when we suddenly stepped up close to Dalby and Jane, the place became terrifyingly silent. The heckler's question to the apostle Paul in Athens echoed in my ears: "What is this babbler trying to say?" (Acts 17:18).

I don't remember what I said that evening, and I'm pretty confident that Dalby and Jane don't either. That's not important. What was important was that we had broken something of a "sound barrier." A precedent had been set.

Aldo Berndt and I had discussed my participation in Dalby and Jane's wedding. We agreed that what we wanted to establish was that I was not speaking as some religious leader but rather as a spiritual mentor and friend—to communicate our belief in the priesthood of every believer.

In the years that followed, we observed that this was, in fact, the precedent that had been set.

Dan, Kent, Ken, Carol, and Brian pose with newlyweds Jane and Dalby.

PART THREE

1977–1987

CHAPTER 20

FORM AND FUNCTION — NOT JUST FOR ARCHITECTS

THERE IS AN anecdote commonly told about the British Army in the days prior to World War II. A civilian expert had been hired to observe an artillery battalion in an effort to improve their speed and efficiency. He watched a crew of seven soldiers move a cannon into position. Six of the men had a distinct task to perform while the seventh stood at attention doing nothing.

When he inquired as to the reason for this man's inactivity, no immediate answer was available. After some research into army history, it was discovered that his role was to hold the horses so they would not run off when the weapon was fired.

When the horses were replaced by a jeep, that soldier's task — his function — was eliminated. But the organizational structure — the form — was left in place because "that's the way we've always done it."

Human history is laced with stories like this that illustrate how a form, a way of doing something, outlives the function for which it was created. In the process, the form often becomes corrupted and abused.

Remember the incident from the Old Testament in Numbers 21 when the Israelites were dying off from a plague of serpents? Moses provided them with a "form" for deliverance. It was a replica of the serpent, made of brass. God healed anyone who had the faith to look at the brass serpent that Moses erected in their midst.

But the story doesn't end there. Generations later, that piece of sculpture had acquired the name of Nehushtan and had become an idol to which the decadent Israelites burned incense. The form had outlived the function and was now corrupted. In 2 Kings 18, a twenty-five-year-old king named Hezekiah "did what was right in the eyes of the LORD" and "broke into pieces the bronze snake Moses had made" (verses 3-4).

That seems to be a common fate with methods. Though they may be inspired by God at the time, they have a tendency to outlive their usefulness. We cling to them long after they should have been discarded, and their proper name at that point becomes a "sacred cow." We could probably use more modern-day Hezekiahs with the courage to do what is right in the eyes of the Lord! But sacred cows don't travel well. When transported from one culture to another, they are not only ugly but often hinder or even contaminate the communication of the gospel.

We first observed this in Curitiba when we translated a small Bible study booklet that was widely used by ministries of The Navigators in the United States to help new believers. The booklet employed a common Bible study method of asking a question, providing a biblical reference where the answer could be found, and giving a few blank lines to write one's response.

The first few times we tried to use this material with students, we got strong, negative feedback. "This is like playing cards with a stacked deck. You ask the question. Then you tell us where to find the correct answer." "Feels too much like what we did in catechism where the church asked all the questions and provided only one set of answers."

Bible study was the function. It was an essential function to meet the needs of educated young people who were basically biblical illiterates. What we needed was a method of study, a form that was appropriate to their style of learning.

The form that evolved consisted of a process that began with a discussion to identify the issue or the key question. Often we would list a series of related questions. For example, a big issue was the subject of money. Typical questions related to accumulation of wealth, was money evil, indebtedness, borrowing, lending, giving, or tithing. Once the questions were identified, Jim and I would assemble a list of scriptural passages, not just isolated verses, that spoke to these issues. It was a biblical bibliography that the students could use for their research.

When we gathered for our discussion, all we needed to ask was "What did you discover in these passages?" In dealing with some subjects the discussion would go on for hours and often extend over a period of several weeks. At the end there were "if, then" discussions around this question: "If this is true, how then should we live?"

We ran into a similar problem when we tried to introduce Scripture memory using the small cards that had become a trademark of The Navigators in the United States. Those cards, which measured 2¾ by 1¾ inches, came into existence when Dawson Trotman, the founder of The Navigators, was trying to get sailors on board U.S. Navy ships to memorize and review verses of Scripture. Those packets of cards were that size so that they could fit into the tiny breast pocket of a sailor's uniform. Now here we were, thirty years later, trying to get Brazilian students to use those same sized cards. That qualifies as a sacred cow, right?

As we listened to the comments from different students, we soon realized it was more than the size of the cards. It was memorization, period. Many of these students had been subjected to a lot of rote memorization in their primary grades of school. When added to the amount of memorization that had been required in catechism, it was apparent that we were not going to have much success with this "form." It was too much like the "Hail Marys" and the "Our Fathers" they had been forced to repeat, often as forms of punishment.

These early experiences alerted Jim and me to the importance of being extremely cautious as we introduced any method or ministry model. For example, in chapter 9 I described an open study. We specifically created those events held in our homes, which was the form, to provide a casual environment where young believers could invite their curious yet skeptical friends for a wide-open discussion of spiritual issues, which was the function.

Years later we created the Domingão to meet a different and specific set of needs. As a form it survives to this day, but it has undergone significant adjustments as needs and circumstances have changed. The name was dropped when, in some locations, the gathering was shifted from Sunday (*domingo*) to Saturday.

In a similar way, we tried to make it a normal practice to evaluate and revise the way we did things. We celebrated the seventh anniversary of the work in Brazil by spending a week with twenty-six of our most mature people discussing the how and why of the way we did things. Some things got the ax; others were approved or improved. Some of the men complained that they lacked familiarity with the Bible as a whole. In response to that, I put together several hours of content as a Bible survey presentation.

From a nearby construction site I borrowed a two-inch by twelve-inch plank that was about ten feet long. I also borrowed a stack of bricks, and using chalk, I labeled each brick as a book in the Bible. As I began, the bricks were lined up in the same order as the books of the Bible. By the time I finished several hours later, they were in historical or chronological order.

As each brick was moved to its new location, I gave a brief summary of its content. I ended up with two bricks left over, which I had labeled with made-up names like 1 Uzziah and 2 Ahaz. I used them to explain the history of how the books of the Bible as we know them were chosen and why some were left out.

It was a one-time presentation, a form created for a specific need or function. The next day all the bricks and the plank were returned to the construction site. But I became the target of good-natured teasing as my Brazilian buddies gave me an honorary title in Portuguese that would be something like a doctorate in "brickology."

Another area where form and function became a critical issue for us was related to the way we did our planning. By the early 1970s our team, composed of a few full-time staff and some who were still in their professions, gathered several times a year.

To fully appreciate our planning process, it is essential to understand that our meetings did not take place in hotels or around conference tables. We usually met in someone's vacation house at a beach. We'd sit on benches around a wooden table in the kitchen. Normal attire was bathing suits; T-shirts were optional. It was casual with a capital *C*.

Elísio, from Florianópolis, was the team comedian. I was bothered at times, thinking that he didn't have a serious bone in his body. I was wrong. It was just that they were Brazilian bones, not bones made in the USA. At one of our meetings, as we were all seated around a table engaged in some heavy discussion, Elísio got up and headed toward the bathroom. He paused en route to pick up a dog-eared copy of a Mickey Mouse comic book, his favorite reading material. He left the door to the bathroom open and, moments later, called out some wisecrack contribution to the discussion that put us all into gales of laughter. It took a coffee break to restore any sense of decorum.

With that as a backdrop, it may be easier to understand the difficulty we faced, beginning in 1970, when the leadership of The Navigators in the United States adopted a method of management known at that time as Management By Objectives, or MBO. This method was instituted in every country where The Navigators was working as part of a global strategy. Planning and evaluation were the functions; MBO was the form.

Jim returned from a meeting of The Navigators' International Leadership Team held in Colorado Springs with the MBO material stuffed in his briefcase. At our next meeting at the beach, he introduced the method and walked us through the planning process. It was tough going.

Part of the problem stemmed from the need to place people in categories with labels—for example, converts, disciples, disciple makers, makers of disciple makers. Each category had defining criteria, such as the number of Scripture verses memorized, the number of Bible study booklets completed. Those categories worked well for ministries in the United States, but it did not fit in Brazil. It was like trying to determine a person's height in feet and inches using a metric tape measure. It required some kind of conversion table.

The Brazilians struggled with categorizing their friends. "Is Carlos a disciple or a disciple maker?" "Jorge is my friend. Do we have a category for friends?"

The core issue centered on the fact that, like so many people in the world, Brazilians are highly relational. Once we asked them to place their friends into categories and start counting them, their friends became a form of currency. As such they became the measure of "success" in the ministry. The temptation, then, was to manipulate rather than serve the people around us so they could be counted or moved into the next category.

At the end of that school year we had a team meeting at the beach to talk about the MBO plans we had written months earlier. Again we agonized, "Was Roberto now a 'disciple maker' or still just a 'disciple'?"

One of the guys had precisely followed the process. He was able to rattle off the numerical objectives he had achieved. The next guy had no numbers at all in his report. Instead he just told stories about some of the people he had spent time with during the previous months. After sharing reactions and feelings for several hours, someone around the table nailed it. Probably it was Elísio. "What this process requires me to do is transform all of my friends into objectives. I can't do that."

It was obvious to us that pursuing this method of planning would change the nature of the work in Brazil. It would become professional, impersonal, and destructive to relationships. Aware of the damage being inflicted, Jim went back to the next International Team Meeting and explained that he would be unable to supply the statistical information the MBO process required.

"Why not?" the men on the team wanted to know.

"Because these people perceive themselves as a circle of friends, not as a ministry or part of an organization."

Not convinced, they persisted. "You know the difference between a convert and a disciple. Why can't you just look around, do a tally, and send us the numbers?"

Jim's answer drew a line in the sand that was absolutely crucial to the future. "I could do that, but not for long. At some point in the future, I'll have to ask a Brazilian, like Aldo, to take over and do it for me. Then he will ask, 'Why do the people in Colorado Springs need to know how many friends we have?'"

That dialogue drove nails into the MBO coffin as far as Brazil was concerned. The office in Colorado Springs continued to gather numerical information and generate MBO reports for ministries of The Navigators around the world. The page for Brazil was left blank.

We reverted back to our "Brazilian" method. This began with lists of our friends, some who were reading the Bible with us and some who weren't. Another list would be of those who had responded to the message and were growing in their faith. We shared stories of what was happening in the lives of these folks: joys, sorrows, weddings, new babies, job changes.

Phase two of the planning process had to do with talking about the needs in the lives of these friends. What was it that would help them move forward in their search for and their relationship with God? And, finally, how could we as a team help one another to best meet these needs?

This was a functional planning process. It was a simple cycle of an action, followed by observing and reflecting on the result of that action. Then we'd think about if and how that action should be repeated. Most important, it was a form that was compatible with the relationship-oriented Brazilian culture.

After a few years, The Navigators discontinued their use of MBO. It was determined that this was not a management form that served the essential planning functions for a culturally diverse organization.

For those of us in Brazil, it underscored the fact that all of life revolves around forms and functions. When the form appropriately serves the function, we hardly notice its presence. But when the form doesn't adequately fit the function, we experience tension and frustration. Or worse, we find ourselves trapped in an out-of-date form, pointlessly standing at attention, holding nonexistent horses.

Jim Petersen leads a beach house team meeting.

CHAPTER 21

THE FIVE As

THE DOORBELL RANG. Carol called out from somewhere at the back of our recently purchased three-bedroom home in a Curitiba suburb, "There's someone at the front gate. Ken, can you see who that is?"

For most Brazilian homes a doorbell is really a gatebell. If there is no bell, the visitor stands at the gate and claps his hands. It would be impolite, even dangerous, to open the gate and come to the front door. The danger would be a welcoming committee formed by a couple of Dobermans. At our home the welcome would come from an overly friendly poodle with muddy paws.

I peeked through the curtains, then yelled back to Carol, "It's Flávio Lazzari and Mario Pudell. Can you make some coffee?" Waving them in, I opened the front door and ushered them into our living room, and we began to talk.

It was July of 1977. We had recently returned from a six-month visit to the United States. While we were away, our role in the ministry in Curitiba had once again been taken over by the Brazilians. That is the sort of occupational hazard you hope for in missionary work. But Carol and I had been wondering and talking about what our next contribution might be. We were about to find out.

Flávio, Mario, and I were still just chatting when Carol joined us a few minutes later, bringing a tray with freshly brewed coffee and some of her world-class chocolate-chip cookies. Watching the two of them go after those cookies raised the question in my mind, *Do guys like Flávio and Mario really come to talk with me, or do they drop by to visit with Carol and see if she has any of her cookies to go along with the coffee?*

On this particular day they wanted to talk with both of us. In addition to being a role model as a homemaker and mother, Carol was spending time with some of the guys' girlfriends, fiancées, and young wives. Her contribution to the conversation that day was significant.

During his final year of high school, Flávio had been a participant in that Saturday night group in Pato Branco led by Dalby that you read about in chapter 19. By the time he moved to Curitiba to begin university, he was an exuberant follower of Jesus Christ. Flávio's personality was heavily flavored by his Italian roots, and I often called him the "Italian Stallion." He was the eldest son in a family of three boys and three girls. Eventually his entire family would come to faith in Christ.

Mario had been raised in a wealthy family from the western part of the state of Paraná. Tall, lanky, with reddish-brown hair and freckles, he was a typical farm boy with a captivating "ah, shucks" sense of humor. At that moment there was no way that I could have imagined where my friendship with Mario would take me.

Flávio and Mario had been classmates for four years and had graduated in December of 1976 with degrees in agricultural engineering. They were now both employed by the state agricultural department. Mario had married his lovely sweetheart, Elizabeth, in June. Flávio and his fiancée, Sonia, were planning a December wedding. Having participated in our Sunday events for graduating seniors, Flávio and Sonia were eager do something together with Mario and Elizabeth.

Even though Flávio and Mario had known each other for several years, it was not until their final year that a close friendship developed. During a month-long agricultural field trip to the north of Brazil, they were roommates and engaged in long conversations about life. Mario's family background was Catholic, but with a heavy involvement in spiritism. As he and Flávio began reading the gospel of John, the person of Christ took over Mario's life in a powerful way. In the context of the growing friendship between the two couples, Elizabeth's curiosity soon had the four of them reading the Bible together.

Once they opened their lives to Christ, Mario and Elizabeth began to realize the conflict that awaited them as soon as he graduated from university. His family had financed his university studies and was expecting him to assume a management role in the family-owned farms back in his hometown. Moving back into a family-run business so heavily influenced by spiritism was something he knew he had to avoid. So he had accepted a low-paying government job in Curitiba, much to the consternation of his family.

By the end of our conversation that afternoon, we had agreed to meet again a few days later to pursue the idea of starting a study group for couples. Carol suggested they come with Sonia and Elizabeth for a soup supper. The cold winter evenings in Curitiba provided Carol with the opportunity to perfect her soup-making skills. Her soup suppers had become something of a tradition for guests in our home.

As the six of us chatted around our dinner table that evening, we agreed that we needed to add a few more couples to the group. When we met again a week later, there were ten of us: Flávio and Sonia, Mario and Elizabeth, Roberto and Maria, Miguel and Claudete, Ken and Carol. This group was about to embark on an amazing, life-changing, precedent-setting adventure. We were to experience hours of fun, moments of great joy, stimulating discussions, mutual encouragement, significant personal growth, and days of heartbreaking sorrow together.

These four couples were a cross-section slice of the ministry in Brazil. Flávio and Mario were agronomists. Sonia was doing postgraduate work in biochemistry. Elizabeth was a talented artist studying oil painting. Miguel was a business administration major at the university while Claudette was an executive secretary. Roberto had a degree in civil engineering and worked for a construction company. Maria was in her final year of school, studying chemistry.

For Carol and me, this was not just one more Bible study group that we would be hosting. Rather, it was a prototype, a living laboratory of which we were a part. As the ministry in Brazil continued to grow, there was a corresponding demand for some kind of cell-type small group to meet their spiritual needs.

I had been reading books, asking questions, and gathering ideas and information about cell groups and house churches. Most of what I had found was not very helpful. The small group movement in the United States was aimed primarily at meeting the needs of members of a traditional church. Much of the material I had studied on cell groups described a traditional church model shrunk down to living room size. These concepts were relevant for people who had grown weary of the large, impersonal gathering they were accustomed to on Sunday morning, but they were irrelevant to these university-educated young Brazilians with limited or, in many cases, no exposure to the institutional church.

While in the United States during the first six months of 1977, Carol and I had served as "missionaries in residence" at Mercer Island Covenant Church in the Seattle suburb of Mercer Island. More than just benefiting from the congregation's gracious hospitality, we were given an insider's view of the church's activities and ministries.

Now that we had unpacked our bags and settled back into life in Brazil, we began sifting through what we had learned as missionaries in residence. We concluded that what made this church such a unique place was not its new state-of-the-art building or its people-friendly sanctuary. Neither was it the upbeat music or Pastor Palmberg's stimulating and thought-provoking sermons. It was more subtle, like the soft aroma from a scented candle or the perfume from a rosebush in full bloom. It was an atmosphere that was hard to define, even harder to explain. But we knew that it had something to do with relationships.

As Carol and I thought and prayed about this newly formed group, we agreed that we wanted to create a similar atmosphere, an environment that would be built around relationships.

In March and April of 1977, I had repeatedly pored over the

content of John 13–17. I was impressed that, in what appeared to be some of Jesus' final instructions to his disciples, the focus was on relationships, not organizations or methods. Jesus' words as recorded on those pages stressed the absolute necessity of quality relationships among his disciples and himself, with one another, and finally in the world in which they lived.

The question that began to form in my mind was "What kind of an environment, what kind of structure will best meet these needs?" A secondary question was "What are the essential relational components needed to live as a follower of Jesus Christ?" I already knew that the answers had nothing to do with pews, pulpits, choir robes, or stained-glass windows.

Carol and I had lived outside the United States long enough by this time to know that the churches we had grown up in were layered with traditions and practices. For example, our Sunday schedule began with "Sunday school for all ages" at nine forty-five. The eleven o'clock hour was sacredly reserved for the morning worship service. Youth groups met at six in the evening, and an evangelistic service was held at seven thirty. The adherence to such a Sunday schedule, along with attendance at a Wednesday evening prayer meeting, was the criteria for determining a church member's spiritual authenticity. While these things had meaning and value in those settings, they were irrelevant to our circumstances in Brazil.

We now faced the challenge of separating that which represented centuries of accumulated cultural baggage from the essential components of a community of Christ followers. The questions we were asking ourselves focused on the needs of these educated, urban-dwelling Brazilians and their particular cultural context.

It was a no-brainer to conclude that if we were working with a tribal people in the heart of the Amazon rain forest, meeting at eleven o'clock on Sunday morning and sitting on pews in a building with a steeple and a cross on top were not essential. What, then, should be the least common denominators around which we should gather in some of Brazil's largest metropolitan areas?

The time we would be spending with these four couples for the next few months put us on a learning curve to answer these and other questions. When we met for the first time, my notes were scribbled in pencil along with some doodling on a scrap of paper dated "26 julho 1977."

Our discussion began around the Portuguese word *ambiente*, "ambiance" in English. It's a word that *Reader's Digest* might use in one of its vocabulary tests. Architects, designers, and decorators use the word frequently to describe the look and feel they want for the space being created in a home or an office. For our discussion it served as the framework for the environment we wanted to create for our group.

We wanted this ambiente to be a place where our nonbelieving friends and relatives could come and feel comfortable. We wanted it to be so attractive that they would be just a bit envious and say to themselves, *I wish I could be part of a group like that.* Just as a decorator would want to furnish a living room to make it warm and welcoming, where you could flop down on the couch and feel right at home, that was the ambiance we wanted for our group.

At the top of our list was friendship, *amizade* in Portuguese. Even though Brazilian culture is highly relational and the ten people in the room had known each other for several years, we agreed that our friendship was somewhat superficial. We knew very little about one another, our family backgrounds, our childhoods.

We immediately agreed that to get started, we would devote time in our weekly meetings to hearing each other's life story. This was a first-time experience for these young people. As they told their stories, in many cases, they were telling things about themselves that they had never felt safe to reveal to anyone before. The three newly married couples learned new things about their spouses. Both Carol and I had been raised by godly parents, and details of our growing-up years prompted curious questions. The result of our sharing was an immediate bonding to one another that was almost palpable.

We agreed that one of the major reasons for superficiality in a friendship is the fear of rejection. If I let someone know the more personal details of my life, he or she may no longer want me as a friend. That led us to add the next characteristic we wanted in our ambiente, which was acceptance. *Aceitação* was the third word beginning with the letter *A*. We laughed and carried on with our discussions.

Real, meaningful acceptance was to become a crucial issue for the group. Initially we were all sweetness. The couples would snuggle on the couch, holding hands and exchanging kisses during our discussions. But then certain habits, mannerisms, and behavioral patterns became irritants. For example, we decided we would start at eight and end at ten each night. One couple consistently arrived late. When confronted with the fact that they were keeping the eight of us waiting, a heated discussion erupted.

Arriving on time is a relevant issue in Brazil's culture. A prompt, on-time arrival at a social event, such as a party or a dinner in someone's home is a major faux pas. Showing up thirty minutes to an hour "late" is the norm. Arriving thirty minutes to an hour late for a job interview or a business appointment could prove to be an economic disaster. If you bought a ticket on the ten o'clock bus to São Paulo and arrived at five past ten, you would have missed your bus.

We hammered out an understanding that our meetings were not like a party nor were they a business appointment or a bus departure. Rather, they were a mutual commitment to treat one another with respect and honor. To show up fifteen, twenty, or thirty minutes late for no good reason was to ignore that commitment; it was a lack of respect for the others.

Learning to accept and value one another in spite of our differences was a significant facet in the ambiance we were creating. But it wasn't easy.

The next topic surfaced as Carol and I told stories of the many ways people at Mercer Island Covenant Church had cared for us during our visit in the United States. One of these took place as we were packing our suitcases to return to Brazil. Our three boys had commented about the down vests worn by many of their friends and wondered if they could buy vests to take back with us. I learned from the pastor that some of our new friends at church, Larry and Judie Mounger, owned an outlet store where they sold cold-weather gear, including down vests. We made a hurried trip to the store, and when we walked in the door, Larry was there to greet us, having been tipped off by the pastor that we were on our way.

Larry ushered us from the outlet store to the factory showroom upstairs, where their current line of ski jackets, rain gear, and down vests were on display. Wide-eyed, the boys each picked out a colorful vest, and Larry wrote down their choices on a notepad. He insisted that Carol and I do the same. Forty-eight hours later, the UPS truck delivered a box with our vests, straight from the factory warehouse. A few weeks later we walked into our very chilly house in Curitiba, and the first thing we did was unpack the duffel bag stuffed full of those cozy down vests!

This example of caring for one another's needs became the focus of our discussion. What this produced was a new level of vulnerability, a willingness to talk openly about personal finances and other decisions. But it also challenged us as a group to help others in a more substantial way than we could have done individually.

One such opportunity arose when an employee in Flávio's office tearfully confided that she was in financial trouble and about to lose her home. Her husband had severe health problems and was unable to work. The amount of money she needed exceeded what Flávio and Sonia could provide. When the group heard the story, we all chipped in, and Flávio was able to hand her the cash she needed to save her home. To protect her dignity, he identified the money as a "loan," but without interest, and gave her no stipulation for how it was to be repaid.

Several years later she came with Flávio and Sonia to one of our meetings, explained that her husband was back at work, and handed each of us a check to repay what we had loaned her. In Brazil's inflationary economy, what we received back represented only a fraction of the value we had loaned, but more important, she had received loving care from a very unusual source: her supervisor at work and a group of his friends. The Portuguese word we chose to describe this kind of care was *amparo*, adding one more *A* to our list.

Each week as we met to discuss these things, we were spending time in the Bible. As we read through the book of Acts together, we were seeing examples of each of our *A* words. One thing that stood out was that the early disciples met to share a meal, absorb the apostles' teachings, and spend time in prayer. Seeing the importance of that served to underscore our need for time together in God's Word and in prayer. Not wanting to break our streak of *A* words, we opted for *alimentação*, the Portuguese word for "nourishment."

Somewhere in the process of using those five *A* words to capture these concepts, we adopted "The Five As" as the nickname for our group. Some time later we added a sixth *A* as a result of a very unique evening.

We had gathered around our dining room table for another one of Carol's soup suppers. Under normal circumstances we would have moved into the living room for our time in the Scriptures and prayer. But that evening, we did something we'd never done before.

Carol and Sonia cleared the dishes off the table, leaving only our wineglasses and the bread plate. I reminded the group that Jesus had used these two things on the table in one of his final teaching sessions with his disciples. I then made the following suggestion: "Before we divide and share this bread and drink the last of the wine, I would like us to reflect for a moment and then share how our lives have been affected by what Jesus did for us on the cross."

I could never have imagined what followed, nor will I ever forget it. One by one those young Brazilians, now devoted followers of Jesus Christ, shared from the depths of their hearts. Quietly, with voices choked with emotion, some with tears streaming down their faces, they offered their praise and thanksgiving for what God had done in their lives, for the love and acceptance they were experiencing in their marriages and from the group. We spent the rest of the evening around that table, in a powerful time of worship and adoration.

At our meeting a week later, as we reflected on that experience, we agreed that we needed to add one more *A* word: *adoration*. The Portuguese word is *adoração*.

This experience had a profound effect on me. As I replayed in my mind those very personal and emotional statements of praise and worship, I turned to the words of Jesus in John 4: "Yet a time is coming and has now come when the true worshipers will worship the Father in spirit and truth, for they are the kind of worshipers the Father seeks. God is spirit, and his worshipers must worship in spirit and in truth" (verses 23-24).

The words spoken around our dining room table that evening were words of profound personal truth. They were words that described forgiveness, freedom from guilt, inner peace, transformation, and new purpose in life. They were words of truth offered to God, but what was permanently engraved in my mind was that they were words of worship.

As that Five As group, now having added a sixth *A*, continued to develop, we were ready to understand more deeply what it meant to be bonded together as the body of Christ.

Ken Lottis delivers the infamous "brickology" Bible survey workshop.

CHAPTER 22

ALLELON — IT'S ALL ABOUT RELATIONSHIPS

IT WAS MORE contagious than I could have imagined. As our Five As group continued to meet, word began to spread like a virus among those who had participated in our Domingões.

"Can we be a part of that group you and Carol are leading?" "Why didn't you let us know you were starting a group like this?"

I gave the same answer to anyone who asked this kind of question. "Get four or five couples together who share your interest, and I'll help you get started." Soon two other groups had formed in Curitiba that were similar to The Five As.

That, in turn, forced me to think about how to define the difference between a Bible study group and a cell group like The Five As. For lack of a better word, I began to use *ambiente*.

I have a file folder full of notes, written in pencil on 8½- by 12½- inch sheets of paper, that I used in those days. They focus on fleshing out what we were learning about creating an ambiente. One such note stated that it was obvious there was a fundamental need for "an ambiente that makes it possible for every person to live life in Christ in all of its dimensions."

In that same folder is a transparency for an overhead projector, evidently something I used in a presentation, that states, "An ambiente exists when people are relating around the Scriptures and prayer, when people are recognizing growth in the lives of others in the group, and when people are utilizing their gifts to evangelize and edify others."

Another set of notes defined *ambiente* with more detail, in which key words were defined: "An ambiente *exists* (1) when *people* (2) are *relating* (3) around the Scriptures and prayer in a *spontaneous* (4), *continuous* (5), and *intense* (6) manner."

1. *Exists*: An ambiente does not form itself; it is created. It either grows or dies. It does not survive without effort and attention.
2. *People*: It is essential that they are committed to and share the same motivation values.
3. *Relating*: Significant communication is taking place by speaking honestly and listening attentively. It is not just another meeting.
4. *Spontaneous*: Becoming part of an ambiente is voluntary, something one wants to do.
5. *Continuous*: There has to be some stability and a commitment to the basic composition of the group.
6. *Intense*: This is not a casual or indifferent setting. There is energy; it is active and engages all aspects of one's life.

This developmental process was about to receive a huge boost following a visit to the post office in downtown Curitiba. During the years that we lived in Brazil, our mail was addressed to a *caixa postal*, a "post office box," rather than to our residence. Because of heavy traffic and parking problems in the heart of the city, often days would go by without a visit to the post office to pick up mail.

On this particular day the caixa postal was stuffed full. Included in what I pulled out of the box was a manila envelope from a friend in Minneapolis, Paul Ramseyer, station manager for KTIS, Northwestern College's radio station in the Twin Cities. Arriving home I ripped open the envelope and found a short note from Paul clipped to a Bible study booklet that he had used in a small group.

So far as I can recall, it was the only time Paul ever wrote to me while I was in Brazil. In a recent e-mail exchange he could not recall what prompted him to send me that booklet, filled with his own notations and comments. The author was Dr. Gene Getz, a former faculty member at Dallas Theological Seminary. The study focused on a Greek word used in the New Testament, *allelon*. This word is translated into English as "one another," "with each other," or "one to another."

I cannot describe my reaction as I paged through the booklet. It was as if someone like the apostle Paul, not Paul Ramseyer, had sent me that information. Instinctively, I knew this was exactly what our Five As group needed to dig into.

Setting the booklet aside, I pulled my massive Strong's Concordance off the shelf. Grabbing a notepad I began making a list of every reference in the New Testament that used the word *allelon* in the original language. I edited the list down to forty-eight passages, rolled a sheet of paper into my typewriter, and began typing what was to become one of the most widely circulated Bible study guides in the work of The Navigators in Brazil. (A translated copy of that study is included as appendix A.)

The Five As began working on that "one another" study. We probably spent a whole evening on the first verse on the list, Mark 9:50: "Salt is good, but if it loses its saltiness, how can you make it salty again? Have salt in yourselves, and be at peace with each other."

That passage, coupled with John 13:35, brought into sharp focus the fact that our identity as followers of Jesus is linked to the way we treat one another. "By this all men will know that you are my disciples, if you love one another."

One evening we began to discuss Romans 12:5: "So in Christ we who are many form one body, and each member belongs to all the others." It was as if someone had rolled a live grenade into the room. What did it mean that we belonged to one another? The concept somehow seemed an invasion of our privacy. Finally, one of the young wives, her voice choked with emotion, summed up our discussion: "If I am not doing well in my spiritual life, it is not just me who is being affected. It affects all of you. This is serious stuff."

The references that spoke of encouraging one another, admonishing one another, and showing compassion toward one another produced some amazing experiences in the group. For several weeks Mario had been complaining about his job situation in the department of agriculture. He was bored with paper pusher tasks and putting together statistical tables. Finally one evening we spent time asking Mario questions, letting him pour out his frustrations, and the group then had a special time of prayer. We asked God to give Mario some creative ideas about his work.

Soon after that he had an idea one morning as he arrived at work. He spent the rest of the day on the telephone, gathering current reports on the state's principal crops from the regional offices scattered around the state. This data normally came to him three to four weeks later as part of a monthly report. With that fresh phone data in one hand and reports from the previous year in the other, he produced an up-to-the-minute forecast of what was happening in the state. There was a drought, and everyone from the governor on down was worried, but nobody knew anything for sure. Now, with Mario's creative work, he knew.

He turned in his report, and after looking it over, his boss took it to the secretary of agriculture for the state. He, in turn, immediately took it to the governor. By noon the governor telexed the report to the nation's capital in Brasília, and that evening the details of Mario's report were on the evening news!

The governor then informed the secretary of agriculture that he wanted a weekly report from Mario. Within two weeks Mario was given a raise that doubled his monthly salary. His subsequent reports were quoted by the federal government in Brasília and published in a national newsmagazine, and Mario appeared on local television to explain his reporting process.

As he kept those of us in the group informed, he consistently gave credit to the encouraging environment of the group and God's intervention in his thinking about his work.

As we continued to focus on these "one another" passages, the results were visible in diverse aspects of our lives. It was normal for me to spend personal time with each of the men; Carol did the same with the women; and we frequently met together with the individual couples. We noted that many of the issues we dealt with in those personal sessions were now surfacing in the group. The truth of Romans 15:14 became a reality in the lives of those in the group: "I myself am convinced, my brothers, that you yourselves are full of goodness, complete in knowledge and competent to instruct one another."

A memorable example of this began when one of the men showed up at our home in the middle of the day. He had walked off the job after an argument with his boss. It was not the first time he had done this, and I inwardly groaned as I listened to the same story all over again.

When he finished, I said, "We've talked about this problem before. It seems my efforts to help have failed. Why don't you bring this up with the group next week and get their input?"

"Oh, no, I couldn't do that. They wouldn't understand, and it would be an embarrassment to my wife," he protested.

"I think you may be underestimating your wife and your friends in the group. Give it some thought."

At our next gathering, when the group began to talk about what was going on in our lives, I looked his direction. He refused to make eye contact, so I decided it was one of those times when push comes to shove.

Pointing his direction, I spoke up. "You and I had an interesting conversation a few days ago about your situation at work. Why don't you tell the rest of the group about that and see what they think?"

After a few moments of tense silence and a "thanks a lot" glare in my direction, he hesitantly told his story. The response was not only immediate, it displayed great empathy and discernment. The advice he received was very practical and was followed by a time of prayer. The accountability to the group brought a needed dynamic that changed his behavioral patterns on the job.

During this same period of time, another significant development was taking place within The Five As. It appears in the notes I kept from the time we spent in prayer as a group. Initially our prayer focused on personal issues. Flávio and Sonia asked us to pray for their wedding a few months away. Miguel was cramming for a final exam at the university. Carol and I asked the group to pray for our three boys and the challenges they faced in their schoolwork. Then the names of other people began to appear. Roberto and Maria had us praying for their friends, Carlos and Paulina. Flávio and Sonia were spending time with a couple from his office.

I cannot pin down exactly when it happened, but we began to talk about the need for a way to bring our friends together. We eventually planned and pulled off a family-type gathering on a Sunday that became part of the life of the group. It was built around a cultural custom of a typical extended-family gathering.

Our home in the Curitiba suburb of Santa Barbara had a two-car garage at the back of the lot that we converted into a barbecue and picnic area. It was the perfect place for our get-togethers. The Five As and their friends would begin arriving with their children around ten on a Sunday morning. Coffee, fresh bread, and fruit were part of the welcome, along with the Sunday newspaper. The women would go to work on salads while the men started a charcoal fire and prepared meat for the barbecue.

At the first of these gatherings, we paused briefly and Flávio spoke to the whole group. He told of how we had come together as a group of friends who shared a common interest and some common questions about the existence of God and the spiritual aspects of our lives. Having enjoyed and benefited from our times together, we wanted to include some of our friends.

He then announced that in a few weeks we would be having

another Sunday gathering that would include a time of discussion built around a reading from the Bible. He made it clear that no commitment was required—come if you're interested, drop out if you're not.

The rest of the day was given to putting meat on the grill and enjoying good food in a family-like environment. After lunch the crowd would play cards or chess or gather around the TV to watch a Formula One race or a soccer match. We had a collection of toys, games, and puzzles to entertain children of all ages. Around midafternoon, fresh coffee was served along with some cake or cookies. Someone usually brought a guitar into the circle, which prompted the singing of sambas or Brazilian folk songs. As evening approached, one by one the families headed home. For those who stayed around, there always seemed to be some leftover salad, and the leftover barbecue was sliced for sandwiches.

These gatherings were an adaptation of the Domingão from a few years earlier. They provided a natural and culturally familiar setting for the gospel to penetrate the lives of busy urban people. The usual outcome for The Five As group was that as their friends responded to the Sunday discussions with growing interest, they would form a new group for the purpose of a more intense study of John's gospel.

In September of 1978, we held a weekend conference in a beach town near Curitiba. We took over a resort hotel and used the largest room they had available for our meetings, which happened to be the bar. Some two hundred people clustered in booths around small tables or sat in chairs scattered across the dance floor. The theme of the conference was "Loneliness, the Disease of Modern Man, and the Body of Christ." I was asked to speak on Sunday morning about what we were experiencing in our Five As group.

In a letter written a few days later, I described the weekend:

My message was about 2½ hours long, with a coffee break in the middle. I don't think I have ever spoken anywhere, on any subject, where I got such a reaction. When we stopped halfway through for the coffee break, people came up, some with tears in their eyes, unable to speak. Those who spoke said things like "This is exactly what I have been needing to hear."

I was overwhelmed.

Months later I recorded in my journal that what I had to say on Sunday morning, September 10, 1978, very well might have been my most important contribution to the work of The Navigators in Brazil.

At that same weekend event, Aldo made several defining presentations on "The Body of Christ." The combination of his messages and my report on our experiences in The Five As were a milestone in the history of the work in Brazil.

Carol Lottis works on plans for a women's Bible study.

CHAPTER 23

SEX AND LIES, BRIBES AND TAXES

IN PREVIOUS CHAPTERS I described two things that characterized our activities during those initial years in Curitiba. The first was the way in which we would read through John's gospel with an individual or in a small group. The second was the time Jim and I would spend together every four to six weeks going over the lists of students with whom we were in contact, discussing and praying over what was happening in each of their lives. It didn't take long for patterns to emerge. That's what this chapter is about.

As individuals began to grasp the truth of what they were reading, their reaction to the person of Jesus Christ and his teaching became more evident. These responses were characterized by expressions of awareness that this was not merely some set of religious ideas that could be attached to an existing lifestyle. Rather it was the realization that many of their basic assumptions were faulty and much of their culturally acceptable behavior was being challenged.

This was not the result of an agenda to confront or accuse that we were following; rather it was one of the consequences of the time they were spending in reading and discussing the Bible. It was as if Jesus himself were joining us at that table in our office or our living room, sipping his cafezinho, and speaking from the pages of Scripture. John

15:22 describes it exactly: "If I had not come and spoken to them, they would not be guilty of sin. Now, however, they have no excuse for their sin."

In some cases, the person would walk out the door and never return. Others would disappear for weeks at a time and then suddenly show up to resume where we had left off in our reading of the Scriptures. Most, however, were captured by the holistic beauty of the message as something that would engage every dimension of their lives—their hopes and dreams for love and marriage, for family, for a career, for lasting relationships. All of life could be integrated if a person became a follower of Jesus Christ.

In these next few pages you'll find four examples of how all this played out in real life. The first two—sex and lies—were essential to personal integrity and foundational for marriage and personal relationships. Bribes and taxes were critical in public and professional life. As you will see, we were not immune spectators to these issues but were learning how our own worldview needed to be shaped by Scripture rather than our North American heritage.

SEX

It was late, and I was exhausted. An engineering student and I had just finished another session in John's gospel. He was one of the first with whom I had engaged in this kind of dialogue. The level of mental energy to think, listen, and speak in Portuguese during those first years was beyond intense. That evening had been no exception. In spite of the cool evening in the unheated office, my shirt was soaked with sweat.

We'd been meeting like this for several months in that little downtown office. Each time we finished and he walked out the door, I had no way of knowing if he would come back.

But he kept coming back, with more questions. It seemed that tonight we'd made some real progress. So I asked my standard question once again: "Do you still have some questions that you need to answer before you can make a commitment?"

He nodded yes but remained silent. I waited. After what seemed like an hour, avoiding any eye contact, he began to speak. I could tell by the tightness around his eyes and mouth that this was critical stuff.

"You've been in Brazil long enough to know..." — he paused, looked straight into my eyes, then continued — "to know what it is like for guys like me. About sex. What happens if I believe and accept this...?" He stopped in the middle of his sentence as I signaled with a slight nod that I understood his question.

He was referring to what was a common cultural pattern for teenage boys in Brazil at that time. At some point in his midteen years a boy would, in the company of his father or an uncle or a family friend, be introduced to a prostitute for the purpose of initiating his sexual activity. From that time on he was expected to engage in regular sexual activity as part of a normal health-care regimen that included more typical things such as a proper diet, exercise, bathing, brushing his teeth, and changing his socks.

Now in a mysterious way that I could only attribute to the work of the Holy Spirit, this young man was questioning the propriety of behavior considered to be completely normal in his culture.

"Good question," I responded, trying to appear calm and collected. Inwardly my stomach was in a knot as I realized how much was hanging in the balance at this moment. As Jim and I had learned, rather than attempt to verbally answer such questions, I turned the pages in my Bible to 1 Corinthians 6, pointed to verse 12, and said, "Start here and read the rest of the chapter. See if that answers your question."

"Everything is permissible for me" — but not everything is beneficial. "Everything is permissible for me" — but I will not be mastered by anything. "Food for the stomach and the stomach for food" — but God will destroy them both. The body is not meant for sexual immorality, but for the Lord, and the Lord for the body. By his power God raised the Lord from the dead, and he will raise us also. Do you not know that your bodies are members of Christ himself? Shall I then take the members of Christ and unite them with a prostitute? Never! Do you not know that he who unites himself with a prostitute is one with her in body? For it is said, "The two will become one flesh." But he who unites himself with the Lord is one with him in spirit.

Flee from sexual immorality. All other sins a man commits are outside his body, but he who sins sexually sins against his own body. Do you not know that your body is a temple of the Holy Spirit, who is in you, whom you have received from God? You are not your own; you were bought at a price. Therefore honor God with your body. (verses 12-20)

Silently, as if in a calm before the storm, he read those lines, sat back in his chair for a minute or two, then stood up. He reached out with one finger and flipped the Bible closed. As he started toward the door, he muttered, "That settles it."

"Settles what?" I demanded, hoping to delay his departure.

With one hand on the doorknob he replied, "That settles it. I could never do that." Turning the knob, he started to leave.

The next few words that came out of my mouth amazed me. It was one of those times when I had no idea what to say but knew I had to say something. What I heard myself saying was, "I am glad to hear that you understand that. You are exactly right. You cannot do that . . . on your own."

Pausing to pick up my Bible, I went on. "Next time we get together, I would like us to look at what it says in here about what happens after we open our lives to God's control."

He hesitated only a few seconds, then agreed. "Okay, I'll see you here. Same time. Thursday evening." And he was out the door.

As I listened to his footsteps fading down the hall, I breathed a sigh of relief and a prayer that he would in fact show up just as he had promised.

This was one of many such conversations that dealt in one way or another with the subject of sexuality. These conversations placed us figuratively and literally in a position of sitting alongside our Brazilian friends, reading and listening together to what God's Word was saying to us.

It was a significant part of our learning experience to see that the issues the apostle Paul addressed in his letters were relevant to life in Brazil nearly two thousand years later. These timeless principles would become foundational for their marriages and family life. It was as if we had been given a new set of lenses to read these familiar writings and see things we had never seen before.

LIES

Before I moved to Brazil, I had never given any thought to the way that lies are woven into a cultural fabric. Living in a culture different from the one I had grown up in, I began to see both the Brazilian and American fabrics. Sometimes when we examine a cultural fabric in light of God's truth, it is like looking at the back side of a tapestry. All the loose ends, including the lack of integrity, become visible.

For example, I wondered about the story of Ananias and Sapphira in Acts 5, if in their real-estate dealings they had a culturally acquired habit of lying about the monetary value of their transactions. Peter confronted them with a new reality: "You have not lied to men but to God" (verse 4). In the next few paragraphs of the chapter, the tragic results are recorded in graphic detail.

As we spent time with these young Brazilians who had become followers of Jesus Christ, the notion that the Scriptures could be a "lamp to my feet and a light for my path" was foundational (Psalm 119:105). We gained new confidence that "the word of God is living and active. Sharper than any double-edged sword, it penetrates even to dividing soul and spirit, joints and marrow; it judges the thoughts and attitudes of the heart" (Hebrews 4:12). We were often surprised by the concerns and questions that surfaced in our discussions.

For students, integrity issues centered around typical things such as cheating on exams, copying term papers, or stealing textbooks. On more than one occasion I listened in amazement to stories about elaborate schemes students conjured up to cheat on an exam. Or how an important reference book would be hidden in a library to prevent fellow students from accessing it. As graduation approached, employment opportunities and the job market became very competitive. If a job offer was posted on a university bulletin board, in many cases the first student who read it might tear it down to prevent others from applying for the position.

The notion that more and better education would resolve Brazil's problems was contradicted by one student, new in his relationship with God, with the following observation: "If it were true that a university education really changes a person, then we shouldn't need padlocks on our lockers at school."

I also came to see the way that lying becomes an unavoidable necessity in a lifestyle of sexual promiscuity. The essential component of trust in marriage, and all other relationships, is impossible to achieve when a person has become a chronic liar.

BRIBES

Once a student left university and entered the business world, a whole new set of questions began to dominate our discussions. "My boss instructed me to give a bribe to a vendor and demand a better price. What should I do?" "I am negotiating a big sale for my company. The buyer is hinting that he wants some money under the table to close the deal."

This led us into areas that, in addition to being deeply immersed in the culture, were very complex. We searched the Scriptures, guided discussions, and asked questions on issues such as when should an employee carry out instructions from an employer and when should he refuse, based on conscience.

When translated into Portuguese, the word *bribe* becomes diversified into a variety of words and practices. For someone not raised in the Brazilian culture, it is rather daunting to understand the subtleties.

As we grappled with this and similar cultural questions we became aware of a tendency toward ethnocentrism, which is viewing other peoples and cultures from the perspective of one's own culture. Americans visiting Great Britain often jokingly refer to "driving on the *wrong* side of the road." I heard a tourist in Brazil ask a salesclerk, "How much is that in *real* money?"

The next logical step in such thinking would be for someone in my situation in Brazil to assume that our cultural determination of right and wrong is also the "Christian" one. However, when subjected to examination in light of Scripture, many black and white aspects of one's own culture fade into gray. Carol and I were both raised in religious environments where drinking wine or beer was prohibited. As we adapted culturally in Brazil, we evaluated that prohibition under the lens of Scripture and made some significant adjustments.

I also concluded that geographic location heavily influences one's thinking on such issues. Peter's journey from Joppa to Cornelius's courtyard (see Acts 10) permanently changed his perspective. Jews born and raised in Jerusalem seemed to have a hard time understanding what Paul was dealing with in Antioch. What might appear crystal clear in Dallas, Texas, or Dayton, Ohio, could quickly become blurry in Curitiba or Campinas.

Growing up in America, I was introduced to the practice of tipping whereby money changes hands as a reward or payment for services rendered. Most of us know about tipping a waiter in a restaurant. Frequent travelers know how much to tip a taxi driver, a baggage handler at the airport, or a bellhop in an upscale hotel. This form of tipping takes place after the fact, as a means of showing appreciation or as a reward. In some cases a tip is given with the intent to influence future service or transactions.

It would not be uncommon to inform a waiter that "we have tickets to a concert and would really appreciate prompt service." The implication of such a request is that you will leave a more generous tip. But would you feel comfortable offering that tip in advance to encourage faster service?

I faced a situation similar to this during our first year in Curitiba. We had applied for a permanent visa and had hired a *despachante*, a person similar to a paralegal, to prepare the paperwork and guide us through the process. I followed the despachante, who was carrying a file folder full of documents, into a government office to submit the paperwork.

Just inside the door he stopped and explained, "There are two ways we can do this. We can hand over these documents and within six to eight weeks they will be processed and ready to pick up. Or I can clip this *gorjeta* to the documents"—he showed me a quantity of Brazilian currency that was about the equivalent of three dollars—"and you can pick up the papers in three days. In that case I would add that amount to your bill for my services."

I had heard about this practice, but this was my first encounter with it personally. In Portuguese the word used for this practice is not *suborno*, which describes money being given to do something that is illegal. Rather the despachante used the word *gorjeta*, which is the same word that is used when giving a tip to a waiter. In this kind of situation, you are giving a tip in advance for prompt service.

We had been working on the permanent visa for months. The daily consequences of living under the temporary visas were incredibly frustrating. Realizing I could bring the process to an end in three days by offering a tip in advance or wait another two months, I had to make a snap decision. What should I do? Refuse, based on my North American gut reaction? Or accept this as part of the Brazilian way of life?

I had already abandoned many of my North American driving habits, such as stopping at stop signs, obeying traffic lights, and giving pedestrians the right of way. When approaching a stop sign at an intersection, one either hits the gas pedal or the brakes, depending on the proximity and speed of other approaching vehicles. Likewise it is not necessary to sit at a red light if there are no other vehicles coming through the intersection. After all, you are more intelligent than the mechanical device that turns a light bulb off and on. And if a pedestrian appears in front of you, the horn usually takes priority over the brakes. These are a normal part of driving in Brazil, and failure to adapt is to risk a nasty accident, being rear-ended by the car following you, or another driver swerving to avoid the dumb driver who just stopped at a stop sign.

Now, in the swirling movement of humanity in the lobby of that public office building, I was at an intersection. I had to make an instantaneous decision. Do I hit my North American brake pedal or the Brazilian accelerator?

Moments later my despachante and I stepped up to the counter, and he passed the folder to the clerk, who greeted me by name. Startled, I stared in amazement. The man who had opened the folder, deftly slipped the gorjeta into a desk drawer, and warmly greeted me was a member of the adult Sunday school class at the Presbyterian church Carol and I were attending at that time. I wondered later if he might have even considered my tip as a sign of thoughtfulness and appreciation for his long hours of public service.

This and other similar experiences helped me to understand the complexities that our young Brazilian believers were facing in their business and professional careers. While some issues were clearly of a black and white nature, others fell into that broad area of gray, in which the insight gained from Scripture, wise counsel from friends, and a conscience sensitive to the Holy Spirit had to guide them.

These experiences also taught me that I could not blindly follow my North American–oriented conscience on the assumption that it was always going to be biblically correct.

TAXES

Probably the most serious lack of integrity appeared in the area of taxes. Personal income tax laws were historically full of loopholes and poorly enforced. In the late 1960s the federal government enacted new laws and gradually closed the net on those who tried to avoid declaring personal income. A massive public information campaign on television pictured the revenue department as a lion. After reminding people to file a return and warning what would happen if they didn't, the lion would cut loose with a fierce growl. It was both effective and intimidating, to say the least.

Not wanting to attract the attention of that lion, Jim and I sought advice from a tax accountant that Jim met at a Baptist church in Curitiba. Carrying our financial records and receipts, we walked into the accountant's office. Spreading out two blank tax declaration forms on his desk, he asked, "So how much tax do you think you should pay?"

Jim and I looked at each other and shrugged. We had no idea why he was asking such a question. He finally suggested a number, as I recall, that amounted to about $100. We nodded our approval and watched as he entered that number on the bottom line of our tax returns.

Then using his calculator, he proceeded to fill in each tax return, backward, until he arrived at the top of the form, with a number representing our gross income. Leaning back in his chair with a satisfied look, he handed each of us a pen and pointed to a line, "Sign here." We had just been given a lesson in Brazilian tax accounting!

Those returns got us officially into the lion's system, and we became card-carrying taxpayers with a nine-digit tax ID number. A year later I had befriended the manager of the Price Waterhouse office in Curitiba. He assigned one of his accountants to assist us in preparing our returns following a more orthodox methodology.

Once again, our own experiences were helpful in understanding the degree of relativity and the amount of gray area in personal income tax laws.

It was, however, in business tax laws that the dilemma had even more dramatic implications for our Brazilian friends. The popular explanation was that the government accepted the fact that, as with personal income, businesses were going to cheat on their tax returns. So taxation was excessive to compensate for the expected evaders.

The common practice was that a business had two sets of books. The official legal books were available for tax auditors and usually reflected a modest amount of profit. The second clandestine set of books usually carried the bulk of the cash flow and substantial profit.

It was into such a business that a young man named Luiz Marcos was hired as a bookkeeper. Marcos had begun his faith journey in the company of Mario Nitsche while they were both employees of a bank in downtown Curitiba. Mario was an eyewitness to an event that earned Marcos a promotion from his lowly job as an elevator operator and made him something of a legend in the bank's history.

Mario had boarded Marcos's fully loaded elevator, along with other employees on their way to the top floor for their coffee break. When the elevator stopped at the fourth floor where the executive offices were located, the doors opened and the bank president stepped forward. Marcos raised his hand to politely prevent his entry — "Sorry, sir, but the elevator is full. I'll get you on my next trip." Mario and the other bank employees gasped as the elevator continued up, looking at this brash young man who had just slammed the elevator doors in their boss's face. Three days later Mario got a telephone call from Marcos with the amazing news: "Orders apparently came from the president; I have just been promoted to a better job."

Several years later Marcos took a bookkeeping job that was to literally put his life in jeopardy. He was introduced to the official set of books and soon demonstrated his skills in the way he handled those tasks. Sometime later he was given the additional responsibility for that second set of books, those the tax department would never see. When the next payday rolled around, he found a sizable quantity of cash along with his paycheck in his pay envelope. The check was from the official business, the cash from the "second" business. He learned there were five or six employees involved in running the "second" business, each receiving a quantity of cash, tax free, and thereby compromised and committed to its secrecy.

For the next few months he and his wife were delighted with the additional income. They began dreaming of how they might spend that money. Then something about conscience came up during a discussion in his Bible study group. Those regular quantities of cash in his pay envelope suddenly came to mind. At first it seemed that this was a normal practice in business and of no concern. But as he and his friends wrestled with the issue, Marcos made a courageous decision. After discussing the matter with his wife, he went in to talk to his boss. He explained that he would continue to do his job as bookkeeper on both sets of books but that he could no long accept those cash payments.

His boss was confused, then angry and suspicious. He was concerned that he had a potential blackmailer or whistle-blower working for him. Months of tension followed as other employees learned of what Marcos had done. No one could comprehend the explanation he had given for not accepting that money. What they were doing was considered so normal; his behavior simply did not make sense.

There had to be some other motive. His telephone calls were monitored, including one that he made to Mario, describing what was going on in the office. The reaction from his boss was immediate. "If you report me to the government tax authorities, I will kill you." Marcos knew that this was not an empty threat. His life was in jeopardy.

He continued to perform his job in such a manner that eventually his boss and fellow employees believed his explanation even though they didn't understand it. He demonstrated that he was trustworthy, a rare commodity in the Brazilian business world.

Several years later, a former fellow employee contacted Marcos with an offer that literally and financially changed his life. A new business had been formed, and they wanted Marcos to come on board to manage their financial affairs. They wanted someone they could trust.

Marcos spent the rest of his professional career with that company, guiding its growth and success.

His experience is just one of many such stories demonstrating how this first generation of believers blazed their own trails through the cultural jungle of the business world based on their growing knowledge of Scripture. It also underscores the absolute necessity for people like Marcos to be surrounded by a tight-knit group of fellow believers. There were similar situations where men discovered some questionable business practice in their workplace. Acting without the benefit of friends to help them think through a plan of response, they quickly characterized themselves as quixotic crusaders, losing credibility and in some cases their jobs.

CHAPTER 24

A MATTER OF LIFE AND DEATH

THE FIVE As were winding up a gathering on a warm summer evening in Mario and Elizabeth's tiny apartment in January of 1970. We were sharing prayer requests when Mario pulled up the sleeve of his shirt to show us a dark spot on the back of his left arm.

"My wife wants me to go see a doctor about this spot," he drawled in his typical laid-back fashion. We all laughed, thoroughly embarrassing Beth. Nobody was laughing two weeks later when he solemnly reported that the biopsy indicated skin cancer, malignant melanoma.

At the time, I didn't know the difference between a melanoma and a watermelon, but I was about to learn. Mario's oncologist surgically removed the spot on his arm and the surrounding tissue. When it appeared that the cancer might be spreading, he recommended that Mario consult with doctors in the United States. With very limited fluency in English, Mario came with a request. "I can't make this trip by myself. My family will cover all of your expenses. Will you go with me?" There was no way I could say no.

The next few days were hectic as we made arrangements to travel to the M. D. Anderson Cancer Center in Houston, Texas. Mario's doctor gave me copies of his records and an article on melanoma from the *New England Journal of Medicine*. I needed a dictionary to read the first sentence. It said something to the effect of "metastasized melanoma is associated with a poor prognosis." Once the implications soaked into my medically challenged brain, I put the article aside.

I pulled it out of my briefcase on board a Pan Am 747 as we flew from Rio to Miami. With Mario asleep beside me, I read a few more paragraphs and learned the time frame for that poor prognosis was something like eighteen months. As we nibbled at our breakfast before landing in Miami, I asked Mario a few questions to find out what he knew and what the oncologist had told him about his diagnosis. The knot in my stomach grew tighter as I realized he did not know how serious his situation was.

I don't do well in hospitals. I never asked my mother, but maybe I didn't have a good experience that June day in 1934 when I was born. I can handle maternity wards and seeing new babies. But I quickly learned that M. D. Anderson was no maternity ward.

I tried not to look at the small children with no hair slumped in wheelchairs. I avoided making eye contact with a gaunt skeleton of a man walking toward me wearing suspenders to keep his pants from falling down. I sat next to a well-dressed gentleman reading the *Wall Street Journal* with an IV tube plugged into his arm, hoping that he wouldn't try to talk to me.

It was all I could do to accurately translate for Mario and the string of technicians and doctors with whom he consulted during those days. When we headed back to Brazil, he was optimistic about what he had seen and learned.

Once we were back in Curitiba, I was faced with a whole new set of issues. Carol and I were surrounded by a generation of young believers, young families like Mario and Beth, who had a beautiful one-year-old daughter. For them it was unthinkable that God would not cure Mario's cancer.

I found myself digging into the Scriptures for answers to questions I'd never been asked before. During our time in Houston, Mario and I had been reading Paul's letter to his friends in Ephesus. Upon our return to Curitiba, we continued to spend time together, often early in the morning before he went to work.

The content of chapter 1 seemed particularly relevant to us in the way Paul painted the big picture of God's purposes for his readers. When faced with one's mortality, seeing that big picture is an absolute necessity. Verses 11 through 14 became the focus of our attention.

> In him we were also chosen, having been predestined according to the plan of him who works out everything in conformity with the purpose of his will, in order that we, who were the first to hope in Christ, might be for the praise of his glory. And you also were included in Christ when you heard the word of truth, the gospel of your salvation. Having believed, you were marked in him with a seal, the promised Holy Spirit, who is a deposit guaranteeing our inheritance until the redemption of those who are God's possession—to the praise of his glory.

The phrase "the plan of him who works out everything in conformity with the purpose of his will" seemed to reiterate what Paul had written in Romans 8:28: "In all things God works for the good of those who love him."

I needed to remind myself and Mario that "everything" and "all things" included melanoma. God had not forgotten us. He also gave a guarantee—not of a specific life span, but of redemption.

After giving that some thought, I told Mario, "When you were born, the doctor gave your parents a birth certificate. That certificate had no fine print that guaranteed how many years you would live. Had he wanted to, the doctor also could have given your parents a death certificate with your name on it, leaving blank the spaces for the cause of death and the date." As he was prone to do, Mario found that idea to be amusing, and we both chuckled.

In August Mario and I spoke to a large crowd at a Domingão in Curitiba in an attempt to share what we were both learning and to answer some of the questions being raised, such as "Why doesn't God do something for Mario?" "Shouldn't we be praying more intensely that God would heal Mario?" As best I could, I tried to point out that God had already done something pretty significant for Mario and for each of us. He had sent his Son to die on a cross so that we might have an eternal relationship with him. But what most impressed me, as well as those who listened to and observed Mario, was his quiet trust in God.

Immediately after speaking at that Domingão, Mario checked in to the hospital. The next day the oncologist did another surgery on Mario's left arm, attempting to eradicate the spreading cells. A nerve was damaged during that surgery, and from that time on his left arm hung limp and useless at his side.

A month or so later, Carol and I, together with Mario and Beth, traveled to Florianópolis and Porto Alegre. Using the same information we had prepared for the Domingão in Curitiba, we had opportunities with groups of people in both cities to talk about life-threatening illness, healing, and death. We were sailing through uncharted waters with this generation of new believers. In spite of the seriousness of the situation, that trip with Mario was a delight. He would tune the car radio to a station that played Brazilian country music and sing along in a hilarious, slightly off-key fashion.

But the reality was no laughing matter. The melanoma was continuing its relentless invasion of Mario's body. Sometime around the holiday season, a CAT scan revealed spots in his lungs. We made plans for another trip to Houston.

After rounds of exams and consultations, a regimen of chemotherapy was recommended. Mario charmed the staff during the slow process of his first treatment. He seemed oblivious to what was about to happen. It was pouring rain when we left M. D. Anderson in a cab. We made it to the entrance of our hotel before he was overcome by the first wave of nausea. For the next few hours I alternately held him in my arms on the bathroom floor or sat at his bedside holding a tray as he vomited and dry heaved.

Upon our return to Curitiba, we became veterans in the chemo routine. I kept a tray under the front seat of my car for the drive home, warning him not to upchuck on my upholstery. He laughed; inwardly I wept.

Because of their heavy involvement in spiritism, members of Mario's family began attempts to persuade him to consult with a famous medium known for his healing powers. They argued that he had seen the best doctors in the United States with no improvement. There were many stories of miraculous cures performed by this healer, as well as other spiritist "doctors" who believed they were reincarnating famous medical personalities from the past.

Mario sought my encouragement as he tried to communicate with his family. His voice was charged with emotion as he told me, "Even if I knew that I could be healed by this man, I would rather die and remain firm in my trust of God's loving care." I choked up as I realized how Mario's words echoed those of Job: "Though he slay me, yet will I hope in him" (Job 13:15).

As new tumors were growing, Mario's pain reached levels he could not tolerate or treat at home. In early September he entered the hospital for the last time. On the morning of September 7, I received the call I had been dreading. Mario had slipped into a coma. I grabbed my Bible and drove across town to the hospital.

With Beth, Flávio, and a few members of Mario's family, we gathered at his bedside. I held his limp hand, read from the Scriptures, and prayed. As I finished, he seemed to awaken slightly and mumbled what sounded like *vou embora*, "I am going away." A few hours later he slipped away from that pain-wracked body into the presence of the One he had come to love and trust in such a beautiful way.

In the corridor outside his room, a member of his family approached me. "As you know, our family has no relationship to a priest or a minister. You have been our brother's spiritual friend and adviser. We would like you to handle things at the funeral and cemetery." My first reaction was to duck and run, but I looked down the corridor and spotted

Flávio. Then I answered, "Thank you. It would be an honor. But I would like to ask Flávio to help me. He and Mario were best friends, as you know."

Brazil has a twenty-four-hour burial law, so we didn't have much time to prepare. Fortunately, someone had called Aldo, who was visiting relatives in Florianópolis, and he boarded a bus early the next morning, arriving in time to help me and Flávio.

As the crowd jammed into the viewing room, we formed a semicircle around Mario's body as it lay in a simple casket. From where I stood, it was immediately apparent that one side of the room was filled with Mario's family and people from his office. On the other side were The Five As, Sonia holding Beth's hand, and some of Mario's friends from the turma.

I spoke briefly of my friendship with Mario and of his incredible faith and trust in God. Then I read John 11:25-26: "I am the resurrection and the life. He who believes in me will live, even though he dies; and whoever lives and believes in me will never die. Do you believe this?" I looked around the room and repeated that question: "Do you believe this?" The contrast on the faces from one side of the room to the other was something I will never forget.

Mario's illness and death ushered us into new territory. As a small faith community and a new generation of believers, we had been brought face-to-face with death and all of its implications. Paul's discourse in 1 Corinthians 15 took on new meaning as we struggled with the loss of our friend.

My journal entry for September 7, 1981, included these words:

Today my friend Mario Pudell died. As I write these words, a lump forms in my throat; my eyes get watery. I am at the same time both sad and glad. Sad at losing a friend with whom I spent many delightful hours. Glad that he was released from a body tortured by a disease that is the very essence of malignancy. Sad because I lost a friend who had invited me into a rare and unique adventure. . . . We had spent so many hours together, traveling, sitting in waiting rooms, hotel rooms, airports, etc., and as a result accumulated a treasure chest of memories. . . . Now I sit in the evening quietness, reflecting over the passages of Scripture that we had shared together. Like Ephesians 1:14 in Portuguese that uses the word *resgate* for "redemption." It is the word used for rescue. . . . Today God rescued Mario from a sick, hurting body.

CHAPTER 25

WILL THIS ROCK IN RIO?

THE YOUNG MAN sitting across the table in the crowded Denny's was a recent university grad. During his years in school he had been an active participant in a campus ministry. While I was visiting in the Seattle area, he had heard me tell some of the stories about what we were doing in Brazil and had invited me to have breakfast. As I went to work on my over-easy eggs and hash browns, he responded to my simple request: "So, tell me about yourself."

What follows is a composite of his story and similar stories that I frequently heard while visiting the United States in the 1970s and 1980s.

"I majored in computer science, graduated at the top of my class, and was recruited to a job with an incredible salary at . . ." and he named a major company in the computer industry. "I went out and bought a three-piece suit, a pair of expensive shoes, and a fancy leather attaché case. When I walked in that first day, it was like a dream come true. After signing some papers and being photographed and given an ID badge, the HR person introduced me to my work group."

He paused long enough to shake his head, as if in disbelief at his own story, and then laughed. "I would not have been any more out of place if I had been dressed like a circus clown. One of the guys who stepped forward to greet me was wearing bib overalls, no shirt, and beat-up Birkenstocks, and his hair was pulled back in a tight ponytail.

The best-dressed man in the group was wearing faded Levi's with holes in both knees, a wrinkled flannel shirt, and a pair of hiking boots. That was the first and only time I wore that suit to work."

I had lost interest in my eggs and hash browns by this time as I listened to his amazing story. "Nothing that I did or learned on campus had prepared me for that day and the months that have followed. I had assumed that having graduated at the top of my class and been active on a ministry team, it would be easy to share my faith at work."

Taking a sip of his now-lukewarm coffee, he went on. "I quickly learned that everyone in that group had graduated at the top of his or her class from the best schools in the country: Stanford, Carnegie Mellon, MIT. They each had their own beliefs and lifestyles. The bib overall guy is a vegan; one of the gals practices transcendental meditation; there's also a Buddhist and an orthodox Jew in the group. They have politely accepted me and my lifestyle, but there's sort of an unspoken rule that no one tries to push his or her beliefs on someone else."

I understood perfectly what he was talking about. His ministry-team experience on campus typically would have been to meet on a weeknight to "do" evangelism, which usually consisted of knocking on doors in a huge residence hall. If the occupant of one room was not interested or slammed the door in your face, you went on down the corridor to the next door. There were probably five hundred guys in a dorm like that, and sooner or later you would find someone who would talk to you. He came out of those experiences with the understanding that evangelism was an activity that one engaged in, an event in which you participated.

Now my young friend was working with the same group of people in the same nest of cubicles fifty to sixty hours a week. He could no longer "do" that kind of evangelism. It could no longer be an activity or an event; it had to be an integral part of his way of living.

We began to talk about building relationships. It became apparent that in his mind, a friendship was a one-way arrangement that he could use to "share" his faith. If the person did not respond immediately, there was no reason to continue the friendship.

He and his new bride had been invited to a few parties by people from work, but they were uncomfortable in those environments, and it must have been evident. The invitations had dried up. He was wondering if he should start looking for another job.

Our early experiences in Curitiba had helped us to see that our relationships were two dimensional. Our young Brazilian friends became cultural guides, walking us into a deeper understanding of the Brazilian mentality. We paid close attention to the words and phrases they used when speaking of faith-related issues. As we read the Scriptures together, we were able to see familiar stories through their eyes and gain interesting insights.

When Jim and I were making those initial friendships in Curitiba, we were also talking and praying about the other major cities of Brazil, as well as the rest of Latin America. We weren't sure how or when it was going to happen, but we believed that God was going to raise up a generation of new believers who would, in the course of their lives, spread throughout the country and across the continent.

Neither of us was eager to commit his life and the lives of his wife and children to the work among students, year after year, only to watch each succeeding wave of graduates die on the beaches of the real world. The idea of launching this effort among students made sense only if they would be able to attractively live God-centered lives once they finished their education.

For that to become reality, it was essential that what we were doing in Curitiba among students and among the recent graduates be kept exquisitely simple, portable, and transferable. It meant that their lives in Christ needed to be a natural part of all that they did, not just an event they attended one night a week or on Sunday morning. It had to be something people could and would be able to do for the rest of their lives.

So the first big question we faced was "Will this thing rock in Rio and the other major cities of Brazil?"

Rio de Janeiro is characterized by beaches, bikinis, and a laid-back lifestyle. You either relax and hang out with the *Cariocas*, as people in Rio are called, or you don't relate. But Rio is also a political hot spot that frequently erupts into student-led protests and traffic-strangling strikes.

São Paulo, on the other hand, is the most industrialized city of South America, where life moves at a frantic pace. Just about every major corporation, bank, and financial institution in the world can be found here. You either learn to live at that pace or you won't survive.

The gauchos of Porto Alegre are also different, fiercely proud of their independent and unique identity as people who work the cattle ranches. Once while sipping a cafezinho in Porto Alegre, I eavesdropped on a conversation that revealed this mentality. The man standing next to me asked his friend, "Did your daughter marry a Brazilian or a gaucho?"

The mobility of what we had started in Curitiba was a frequent subject that Jim and I talked and prayed about. At some point the word *movement* entered our conversations.

With the help of an attorney, we had registered a legal organization called Os Navegadores do Brasil (The Navigators of Brazil). As a legal entity that organization lived its life hidden in a desk drawer. Os Navegadores do Brasil had no bank account, owned no property, and needed no office with its name on the door. It existed solely for the purpose of providing a legal identity for our presence in Brazil and to help us obtain visas for future arrivals.

A movement, by comparison, is hard to define and doesn't always have a legal existence. It may be organized but lack ties to a single organization. There is leadership but no centralized control.

A classic example is what happened after Dr. Kenneth Cooper published a book, titled *Aerobics*, in 1968, in which he introduced a new word into the English language and a revolutionary concept of physical conditioning. That book has been translated into scores of different languages, and its message has changed the lives of people around the world. Today in the suburbs of Dallas, Texas, the Cooper Aerobics

Center occupies a multimillion-dollar facility located on nearly two thousand acres. Cooper's name is synonymous with aerobic exercise; Brazilians ask one another, "Have you done your Cooper today?"

But the key to Cooper's movement is not in his name, his books, or that state-of-the-art facility in Texas. It is in the simplicity. To join the movement, all you need to do is pull on a T-shirt and a pair of shorts, lace up your tennis shoes, step out the door, and you're a participant.

In a similar fashion, to join the movement in Brazil all you need is to sit down with a friend, grab a couple of inexpensive Bibles published in Brazil by the International Bible Society, and start reading. Maybe add an ashtray and brew some coffee.

Anything more than that has a tendency to become excess baggage.

Sometime in the mid-1970s the use of overhead projectors became a standard practice in schools and businesses. The suggestion was made that the turma in Curitiba should buy a projector that could be used for larger group gatherings, such as a Domingão.

An astute young man, Epaminondas Rosa, objected. "I'll donate some money for the projector," he said. "But it must be owned by an individual, not the turma."

"What's the problem with the turma owning an overhead projector?" someone wanted to know.

Epaminondas was ready with an answer that cut to the heart of what keeps a movement mobile. "Today it is an overhead projector; tomorrow it will be something else. Eventually we will need to have an office to store all this stuff. Next we'll need to hire someone to manage that office. So let's go ahead and buy the projector, but it has to be owned by a person, not the turma."

He understood that in a material world, as beneficial as material goods might be, they can become the excess baggage that slows a movement down and eventually brings it to a complete halt.

MOVEMENT AND LEADERSHIP

From the earliest days in Curitiba, Jim and I had endeavored to hand off leadership responsibilities to our Brazilian friends. Whether it was a weekly Bible study group for a half dozen students or one of those Sunday morning "open studies" described in chapter 9, we preferred to coach from the sidelines rather than keep on doing it all ourselves. It was a trade-off. A less than perfectly led discussion was more than compensated for by the message we intended to send: "This is your thing, not ours."

As mentioned earlier, when one of us would travel to the United States for a furlough, all of his leadership responsibilities would be handed off to Brazilians. When we returned, we cautiously reinserted ourselves into the flow of things, being careful not to pick up where we had left off.

Then in May of 1973 a significant exclamation point appeared behind the word *leadership* when Jim wrote the following letter to some of his friends in the United States:

It took exactly nine years, nine months, and twenty-four days. On August 21, 1963, we landed in Brazil. The assignment was to win some men to Christ, build them up, and produce the leadership necessary to maintain a movement of disciplemaking in this country of 100 million people.

This has been an incredible adventure for us! We now find ourselves surrounded by our great "family" of growing Christians. From among them a very able leadership has emerged—men of real stature who have, in fact, replaced us. Since our presence is no longer necessary, we are packing our bags and have reservations on a northbound Boeing June 15.

We want you to meet our replacement. His name is Aldo Berndt. Aldo is a man of God and a very gifted guy. I have no qualms about placing the ten years we have invested here into his hands.

This doesn't exactly mean we're looking for work. We plan to spend two years in Colorado Springs preparing ourselves and mounting teams to develop the Navigator ministry in the remainder of the Latin American countries. Then we expect to move back to some place in Latin America.

When Jim boarded that June 15 flight, along with Marge and their four children, a set of changes were already under way that gave the work in Brazil a new appearance. A generation of Brazilian leaders was emerging. Osvaldo and Lenir Simões were preparing to leave for a year of cross-training with The Navigators in Mexico. Mario Nitsche was withdrawing from his dental practice so that he and his wife, Sueli, could devote their time to ministry among students. Fernando and Ieda Gonzalez had joined newcomers Ray and Sharon Rice to open a new student ministry in Ribeirão Preto. When Aldo and Aracy moved to Curitiba, they left behind Elísio and Celina Eger leading a growing group of students and recent graduates in Florianópolis. In Porto Alegre, Jack and Barb Combs anchored a maturing team of students and graduates.

Carol and I became not only observers of, but participants in, a process under Aldo's leadership that gave the ministry in Brazil its distinctive aroma and ethos of being Brazilian "owned and operated."

At some point in the history of our time with The Navigators, the language of Matthew 9:37-38 captured our attention: "Then he said to his disciples, 'The harvest is plentiful but the workers are few. Ask the Lord of the harvest, therefore, to send out workers into his harvest field.'"

The King James Version uses the word *labourers* in place of *workers*. Somebody coined the phrase "Laboring for a lifetime," which became our rallying cry. We wanted to see an endless stream of laborers who were equipped and motivated to be engaged with God's plan and purposes . . . for the rest of their lives.

For that to happen, local leadership needed to be prepared and each succeeding generation needed to recapture a passion for articulating the good news in the idiom of their generation.

One of the key components in making this a reality was the way these young families were building their marriages and raising their children. We were asking ourselves, "How can we best equip these families to raise their children in 'the nurture and admonition of the Lord'?" (Ephesians 6:4, KJV).

We knew that top priority had to be given to building a solid marriage. One of the memorable phrases used by our friend and marriage mentor, Dr. Henry Brandt, was: "More things are caught than taught." As related in chapter 19, we were making a huge investment of our time to equip these young families.

Patterns had changed in our own family as we began doing more things on Sunday mornings with students. During our first years in Curitiba, we had attended Sunday school and church as a family. By the time we moved to Porto Alegre in 1970, that had ceased. We were learning that Sunday school didn't need to take place on Sunday morning at nine forty-five in a building with a sign out front that said "church."

On those Sunday mornings when our living room was jammed with students for one of our open studies, our three boys would participate. On more than one occasion, during the question and answer discussion, one of the boys would raise his hand and fire off a question or even give an answer to a question that had just been asked.

Seeing their mom and dad spending time in the Scriptures with a student or a young couple made it seem natural that our boys should get that same kind of attention. Thus there were times when we would hang around the table after dinner and as a family read and talk about something from the Bible. I would often bring to the table a book that I was currently reading. I would read a paragraph or two and then ask some questions to get their reaction. On many occasions I would arrive home, walk into the kitchen, and find one of the boys engaged in deep conversation with his mom. I would offer a quick greeting and exit stage left, not wanting to interrupt what was taking place.

In the years that followed we encouraged a generation of families who "homeschooled" their children in the faith. These kids grew up watching their moms and dads gather with friends in the living room for times of Bible study, prayer, and sharing of life's experiences. That same crowd would gather, along with neighborhood friends and colleagues from work, to watch Brazil's team play in a World Cup soccer match, have a barbecue, or just hang out together.

It seemed significant to me during this period, as I pondered what the apostle Paul was saying in 1 Timothy 3 about leadership, that he included specific references to the home. The overseer in verse 4: "He must manage his own family well and see that his children obey him with proper respect." The deacon in verse 12: "A deacon must . . . manage his children and his household well." And in verse 5 Paul asked, "If anyone does not know how to manage his own family, how can he take care of God's church?"

The family household in that era often included the extended family—uncles, aunts, grandparents—as well as servants and their children. When a husband and wife managed that kind of household well, it became the criteria for making their home the gathering place for other believers, something they called a church.

Preparing local leadership in Brazil did not mean that they needed to have MBAs or be capable of heading up large corporations. But it was very important that they learned to care for one another as husband and wife, and for their children as father and mother.

In our collection of black-and-white photographs of those gatherings in our home and the homes of our Brazilian friends, it is not uncommon to spot our boys mingled in the crowd, a babe in arms, or a toddler peering out from between someone's legs. It should come as no surprise, then, that the idea of passing on one's faith would become a natural part of life, as natural as birthday parties, rice and beans, and a cafezinho.

We were confident that this kind of movement would in fact "Rock in Rio," as well as just about anyplace in the world where people harbored a deep hunger for meaning in life but were no longer looking to religious institutions for answers.

CHAPTER 26

THE PICTURE ON THE JIGSAW PUZZLE BOX

IT WAS THE Christmas season of 1997. Our home in Mercer Island, Washington, was stuffed with people. Using folding tables and pieces of plywood, Carol had stretched our dining room table into the living room and somehow managed to squeeze in places for all twenty of us. I picked my way through the noise and congestion in the kitchen to ask Carol if there was anything I could do to help. I got more than I bargained for.

She showed me her list of the twenty people to be seated around the table. It included Kent and his Brazilian wife, Carin; Daniel and his Argentine wife, Myrna; Brian and his American wife, Annette; and our grandchildren—five at that time. There were also Evilásio and Marilene Gioppo, Brazilian Navigator staff on sabbatical in the United States with their three teenagers who were attending school on Mercer Island. Last but not least were Myrna's parents, Nelson and Chela Iperico, from their hometown of Belleville in the interior of Argentina.

With a twinkle in her eye, Carol said, "See if you can make up a seating chart so that each of our guests is seated next to someone who speaks the same language."

I took her list and added the languages spoken by each person.

Here's what I had to work with:

Kent Lottis: English, Portuguese, some Spanish
Carin Lottis: Portuguese, English, German, Spanish
    Gabriel, age seven: English
    Ian, age five: English
    Nathanael, age five: English
Daniel Lottis: English, Portuguese, Spanish, some French
Myrna Iperico Lottis: Spanish, English, some Portuguese, some French
    Ana Letícia, age eight: English, Spanish
    Paulina Luísa, age four: English, Spanish
Brian Lottis: English, Portuguese, German, some Spanish
Annette Lottis: English
Evilásio Gioppo: Portuguese, some English
Marilene Gioppo: Portuguese, some English
    Carlos Eduardo, age seventeen: Portuguese, English
    Juliana, age fifteen: Portuguese, English
    Carolina, age twelve: Portuguese, English
Nelson Iperico: Spanish
Chela Iperico: Spanish
Carol Lottis: English, Portuguese
Ken Lottis: English, Portuguese

It took some effort, but I eventually managed to seat every person by someone who spoke his or her language. There was no lack of conversation during the wonderful meal, even though there were usually three languages in use at the same time.

After dessert and coffee, we set up a card table in the middle of the living room. We opened a gigantic jigsaw puzzle and dumped its pieces in the middle of the table. What happened over the next few hours made a profound and lasting impression on me. After studying the picture on the puzzle's box, our guests began to sort the pieces by color with little or no verbal communication. Some of the pieces were shifted to a nearby coffee table, dividing the group into two separate teams.

Throughout the afternoon, people wandered in and out of the living room, pausing to observe progress on the puzzle or stopping to join the search for a needed piece. I watched, fascinated, as seven-year-old Gabriel worked silently beside Myrna's sixty-three-year-old father, Nelson. They exchanged glances, gestures, and nods to communicate. The three Brazilian teenagers chattered away in a mixture of Portuguese and English as they toiled alongside Brian and Annette.

But the one thing that continued to happen over and over again was that the polyglot group of puzzle workers would pause in their labors to look at the picture on the box. Sometimes it was just a quick glance. Other times it was to intently study, while holding a puzzle piece in hand, trying to locate where that piece fit into the bigger picture. On several occasions three or four people would pause to focus their attention on the picture while they discussed what to do next.

Age, nationality, and language differences did not prevent people from working together on a common task as long as they had the picture on the box to guide them. Seeing the big picture was a must, an absolute necessity. Over and over again.

The experience that afternoon in our living room helped me understand what had taken place during our final years in Brazil. During the mid-1980s I was spending more and more of my time showing people the picture on the puzzle box. That picture, of course, was the kingdom of God.

I noted with particular interest Paul's activity as described in Acts 28:30-31: "For two whole years Paul stayed there in his own rented house and welcomed all who came to see him. Boldly and without hindrance he preached the kingdom of God and taught about the Lord Jesus Christ."

While I was not under house arrest, as Paul was, it was apparent that while the nature of my ministry contribution had narrowed, the scope of activity had widened. Taking my cue from Paul's job description in Acts 28, I seized every opportunity to teach about the person of Christ and his kingdom.

After that experience in our living room, I realized that on these occasions I had been holding up the image on the puzzle box, the kingdom of God, and trying to help people see how all the pieces fit into the big picture of God's plan and purposes and, more specifically, how they were a part of that image.

Whether it was a gathering of people in a living room, a small cell group like The Five As, or one-on-one time with an individual, we would read and then discuss some of the New Testament sections that begin with the phrase, "The kingdom of God is like . . ." I would ask questions such as "What do these verses say about how we should think and live as citizens of the kingdom?" "What are the unique kingdom values that are portrayed here?" "How does this piece fit in with the others?"

To illustrate the necessity of seeing the big picture, I made up a story about some Brazilian tourists who traveled to the United States but only visited Disney World. Even though they had been in Florida, they had never seen the Everglades or visited Key West. They were not interested in visiting Washington, D.C., seeing the Grand Canyon, or driving across the Golden Gate Bridge. Their photos and postcards were mostly of Mickey Mouse, Donald Duck, and the hotel swimming pool.

While that story always got a lot of laughs, it was painfully close to reality. Brazilian travel agents sold a lot of excursion packages to the United States that consisted of a round-trip to Orlando, a bus ride to a hotel near Disney World, and then a few days later, a ride back to the airport.

When Jesus spins out story after story about the kingdom, it is as if he is showing us snapshots and postcards of the uniqueness and diversity that his kingdom embraces. And like the pieces of a jigsaw puzzle, they need to be assembled as one looks at the big picture in order for them to be understood.

Too often, like my hypothetical Brazilian tourists, we have a tendency to lock in on one or two snapshots of something, like our local church or a particular doctrinal issue, and never see the big picture, the kingdom of God.

My concern then, as it is now, was that the movement in Brazil would lose its impetus after the first or second generation. So during those final years, I tried to keep the focus on the big picture.

It was like the evening Carol and I spent in Rio de Janeiro. We traveled there to visit Miguel and Claudete, who had been part of The Five As before they moved to Rio to start a business. Now they were leading their own group, composed of five couples. Four of the couples were new believers, and the fifth was brand new to the group, still checking things out. Jammed into the tiny living room of a high-rise apartment, I wound up seated on the floor, leading a discussion about what a marriage should look like in the kingdom culture.

Suddenly, after an hour or so, the young husband seated next to me broke in, "Okay, that's it. Stop; don't say anymore. I've heard all I need to hear for one night." At first I thought he was upset, but then I realized he was just really excited about what he'd been learning and said so. Twenty-four hours later he and his wife were back, ready for more.

We also conducted a series of workshops for couples who were leading cell groups in their respective cities. The notes I prepared for leading those events always included a block of time to listen to what these people were dealing with in their groups. I wanted to be sure that we were addressing the issues they and their friends were facing in their careers, in their marriages, and with their children. I also wanted them to know that they were not alone, that others were dealing with the same challenges.

We would also dig into the Scriptures to trace the spread of the gospel and to notice the role that families played in carrying out Matthew 28:18-20. It was the "households" that constituted the foundational building blocks in each city. Similarly, I was convinced that the success or failure of this movement in Brazil was linked to the families. If the children growing up in these families were not impregnated with a kingdom-oriented way of life, the movement would be nothing more than a short-lived phenomena that affected only a single generation.

One of the ways we had observed kingdom culture moving across generations took place as students lived and shared their faith with their own parents. During our final years in Brazil, we participated in a unique experience that had its origins in the student ministry in Curitiba led by Dan and Suzanne Greene.

The Greenes arrived in Brazil in the mid-1970s to join the Brazilian Navigator team. They brought fresh initiative to the student ministry in Curitiba. Our three sons—Kent, Daniel, and Brian—were involved, taking their friends to open studies and parties at Dan and Suzanne's home. These students eventually began meeting regularly on Sunday evenings for a freewheeling, wide-open Bible reading and discussion group.

During a party held at our home, I got into a conversation with one of Brian's friends, Janete Andrade. She described a problem she and some of the others in this group were facing. "My parents and the parents of most of the others in the group are really curious, even worried, about our Bible discussions. They know Americans are involved, and that adds to their concerns."

"What do you think we should do about this?" I asked. Knowing Janete, I was pretty sure she already had a plan in mind. She did.

"All of us in the group could invite our parents to a Sunday barbecue. We could have it at our place. Then, as parents, you and Carol could describe exactly what it is that we do in our discussions and answer any questions they have."

Janete's parents, Benedito and Narita Andrade, lived next door to her grandparents, the Stoccos. They shared a big backyard with a nice picnic area and agreed to host the event. When the idea was announced to the group, everyone pitched in to make it happen.

The weather cooperated, and it was a crisp, sunny winter Sunday morning as the crowd arrived. It was a bit awkward at first, as most of these people did not know each other. But once the grilled sausage appetizers started coming off the grill, the noise level of conversations increased. The oft-repeated phrase we'd learned, "Brazilians know how to party," was proven to be true once again.

Among those present was Vanessa, a girl our son, Kent, was dating at the time. She introduced us to her parents, Gildardo and Otília Tomich. Gildardo and I were seated side by side in the Stoccos' rather cramped living room as we sipped our after-meal cafezinho. We had discovered some common interests in the books we liked to read and were immediately on a track to become close friends.

As hostess for the event, Janete quieted the crowded living room full of people and introduced Carol and me to the group. As I stood up to speak, I was aware that the pope was looking over my shoulder. Janete's family were devout Catholics, and a large framed portrait of Pope John Paul II hung from the wall behind me. I thought to myself, *Don't screw this up, Ken. The pope is watching.*

I need not have worried. The students had been praying for this gathering, and the atmosphere was warm and open. I briefly described what we had come to Brazil to do and stressed our emphasis on becoming personally familiar with the Bible rather than converting people to a new religion. I wound up talking about the historical person of Christ and his kingdom.

Then, because the students had suggested that I do so, I closed with an invitation: "If you are interested in knowing what your sons and daughters do in their Bible discussions, two weeks from today, at our home, we're going to do the same thing we did today, except it will just be us, as parents. We'll enjoy some good food, have some dessert and coffee, and then open the Bible together and read the first chapter of St. John's gospel. So let us know if you'd like to do that."

When I asked if there were any questions, the momentary silence was broken by a friend of Brian and Janete, a member of a musical group in which the three performed. This man had studied for the priesthood in Europe, and from previous conversations I knew that he was a real thinker. He launched into a long introduction to his question that was loaded with theological terminology. I struggled to follow his line of thought. Then he finished with, "So if I understand what you've told us, you are not interested in promoting historical Christendom, but rather in directing young people to discover the person of Jesus Christ and his kingdom. Is that it?"

Relieved, I nodded. "Yes, that's it exactly."

Two weeks later nearly every one of those parents showed up for what was the first biweekly gathering of a group that went on for several years. Initially, as was to be expected, there was a certain timidity during the discussions. These were people in our age group who had grown up in the Catholic Church, with little or no personal exposure to the Scriptures. Gradually they came to realize that the others in the group were similarly limited in their biblical knowledge, and they no longer were afraid to ask questions.

One memorable such breakthrough occurred in our second gathering. We were working our way through the second half of John 1. I asked one of the men to read verses 29 to 34. Being a retired army officer, he rose from his chair, stood stiffly at attention as if reading orders to his troops, and began to read, "The next day John saw Jesus coming toward him and said, 'Look, the Lamb of God, who takes away the sin of the world!'"

When he came to the end of that line he stopped. He stood silently, staring at the Bible he held in his hands. Then he looked up and exclaimed, "So that's where that comes from." He was referring to the phrase that is used in Mass, "O Lamb of God, that takest away the sins of the world, have mercy upon us."

He stared again at the open Bible. I watched his lips as he silently reread the words, "Lamb of God, who takes away the sin of the world." What he said next brought tears to my eyes.

Looking around at the rest of the people in the room, he spoke in a near whisper, amazed at what he had just discovered. "So Jesus is the Lamb of God."

The next few years with the parents of our boys' friends and classmates proved to be one of the major highlights of our time in Brazil. It was the first and only time that we were able to develop friendships with people in our own age group.

Beyond that was the opportunity to be participants in seeing the good news of the kingdom move "upstream." It is more common that the gospel moves "downstream" from parents to their children. It is a rarer thing when the power of the kingdom message flows upstream from the children to their parents. That's what can happen when the kingdom culture is first affirmed and then proclaimed. To skip over the affirmation and start preaching is a recipe for damaging family relationships.

Keeping the picture on the puzzle box—the kingdom of God—close at hand and clearly in focus is not an option, it is an absolute necessity.

CHAPTER 27

SORTING OUT
THE OPTIONS

IT WAS A cold winter morning in June. I awoke to the muffled sounds of conversation from the kitchen where Carol was making coffee and fixing breakfast for Dan and Brian. Determined to catch a few more minutes under the covers, I was drifting back to sleep when I heard a knock on the bedroom door.

Carol cheerfully entered. "Wake up, birthday boy, you have a visitor."

Behind her, carrying a tray with two steaming mugs of *café com leite* (coffee with milk), was Aldo. "*Bom dia, amigo! Feliz aniversário.*" (Good morning, friend. Happy Birthday.)

He had traveled ten hours overnight by bus to spend the day helping me celebrate my fiftieth birthday. As we sipped our café com leite, he delivered a package from Jim Petersen. It was a T-shirt with the phrase "fifty and still nifty" stamped across the front. The shirt had been given to Jim a few years earlier; now it was mine for a few years before I passed it on to Aldo. A good-natured, nevertheless not-so-subtle, reminder that we weren't getting any younger.

Aldo and I spent the day together, and late that night, I saw him off on an overnight bus for the journey home. He had given me an unforgettable birthday gift, a unique and profound gesture of friendship.

During the course of our day together, Aldo talked with Carol and me about what had become the number one topic of conversation for us. We had returned to Brazil late in 1983 after a prolonged stay in the United States. Discovering how to best fit back in to the ministry had been more difficult than on previous occasions. The maturity and spiritual depth of our Brazilian friends were the reasons for this delightful dilemma. There were no immediate or urgent gaps to step into. The word that frequently surfaced in these conversations to describe how I was feeling was *redundant*.

While I was excited about the opportunities described in the previous chapter, we had unanswered questions about the future. Some changes were about to happen that we jokingly referred to as our "musical chair game."

Jim was scheduled to move back to the United States to assume a role in The Navigators International Office. He was in the process of handing off his responsibilities for Latin America to Aldo. Mario Nitsche would then take over Aldo's "empty chair" in leading the Brazil team.

One implication in this transition was that the time had come for me to vacate my "chair" even though it had no title other than my being the old-timer who had been around since day one. In those conversations on my birthday we went over the details of what appeared to be the two options that were on the table.

The first was to team up with Aldo and begin to familiarize myself with the ministries of The Navigators in Argentina, Chile, Venezuela, Costa Rica, and Mexico. This would mean a lot of traveling and require becoming fluent in Spanish. The second option was to relocate to another major city in Brazil and help pioneer a new ministry.

Over the next two years we pursued both of these options. Carol and I made a two-week trip to be with Navigator staff in Argentina. We visited in the homes of each couple to get acquainted with the family and meet some of the people in their ministry. Having spent so many years on our own in Brazil when our children were grade-school age, we knew how lonely it could be. Therefore, we tried to get to know each of the children, asked a lot of questions, and focused on encouraging them in specific aspects of their marriages and child rearing.

I really enjoyed traveling with Carol. Even though I had been in Argentina on previous visits and was familiar with these families, my learning curve went vertical as Carol asked questions and discovered things I had completely missed. It became obvious to me that my effectiveness would be severely limited if I had to make these kinds of trips alone.

Before returning to Brazil at the end of that trip, we spent several days on our own in Buenos Aires. We loved the city, which is often referred to as the Paris of South America. We wandered the streets around our hotel, had lunch in sidewalk cafés, enjoyed elegant afternoon coffee at the Café Richmond on Calle Florida and dinner in a traditional Argentine steakhouse. This gave us time to talk about what we had been doing in the preceding days. While we had no doubt as to the value of this kind of visit, we harbored deep uncertainties as to whether we were cut out to do this kind of traveling long term.

I also did some traveling with Aldo. We made a ten-day visit to Costa Rica in response to an invitation from Navigator staff there. They had a growing number of students graduating from university, and they wanted to learn from our experience in Brazil.

Traveling with Aldo was easy. Fluent in four languages—Portuguese, Spanish, English, and German—he could do all the talking at check-in counters, passport control, customs, and immigration. We worked well together, often being able to laughingly complete one another's sentences.

The days in Costa Rica gave me a preview of what might be ahead. Aldo quickly switched to Spanish and hit the ground running. Prior to the trip I had hired a teacher and worked at adding some necessary Spanish vocabulary and verbs. Spanish and Portuguese are similar; in some cases they share identical vocabulary, but they do not always convey the same meaning. So it was somewhat like walking through a verbal minefield, aware that I could be using a word that would explode, causing confusion or embarrassment. My notes from that trip recorded an example of the latter.

We were staying in the home of Costa Rican Navigator staff, Jorge and Zayra Davila. The first morning I walked into the kitchen and asked Zayra in my best Spanish, "Is there water in the bathroom?" Jorge had told us the night before that there was a local water shortage, and at bedtime there was no water in the bathroom. She replied, "No, you can enter." I was wide-awake enough to know I had failed to communicate but still understood her reply. "There was nobody in the bathroom. I could use it." Great way to start the day.

In spite of my efforts to prepare, it was very difficult to keep up with and contribute to the conversations in Costa Rica. Aldo and I discussed the possibility that Carol and I would need to spend three to six months in a place like San José, Costa Rica, or Guadalajara, Mexico, in order to immerse ourselves in a language-learning situation. That idea, although a very logical thing to do, did not generate a lot of enthusiasm with me or with Carol. Her comment was, "After all these years I find that I am still struggling to understand and be understood in Portuguese. How can I start on another language?"

The other option on the table was for us to relocate to another major Brazilian city and help pioneer a new ministry. Part of that plan got under way when Evilásio and Mari Gioppo moved from São Paulo to Recife, the fifth largest city in Brazil. Situated on the coastline of the continental shoulder that protrudes east into the Atlantic and just south of the equator, temperatures rarely get below seventy-five or above one hundred degrees year-round.

Responding to their invitation, Carol and I flew into Recife to spend a week with Evilásio and Mari. We immediately understood why they were suffering from a mild form of culture shock, even though they were still in their own country. For starters, temperatures in southern Brazil where they had grown up ranged from ninety degrees on the hottest summer day to below freezing in winter.

The rented home they were living in had a wide veranda that faced the street. Their dining room table, along with some of their living room furniture, was outdoors on that veranda. We spent most of our time on the veranda, only going inside the house to prepare meals, use the bathroom, and sleep.

Late in the afternoon on the first day of our visit, we donned our swimsuits and walked the four or five blocks to the beach. As we crossed several busy streets, Carol and I were subjected to whistles, catcalls, and less-than-polite remarks from passing motorists because we were glaringly white-skinned in an area where a year-round suntan is the norm. As we arrived at the white sandy beach, Evilásio led us to a coconut vendor. Seeing us coming, the vendor reached into a tank of ice water and retrieved a green coconut. Balancing it on one hand, he wielded a machete with the other and, with a few swift whacks, cut off the top. Inserting a straw, he handed one of these "cold drinks" to each of us. Delicious!

After a swim in the lukewarm ocean, we headed back to the house to shower and fix dinner. It was late, after nine, when we gathered around the table, having waited for the evening breeze off the ocean to cool things down a bit.

The next few days were filled with long conversations with Evilásio and Mari about the adjustment to what amounted to a new way of life in this tropical setting. We visited the university campus where he was already meeting with some students to read the Bible. The heart of downtown Recife is sometimes called the Brazilian Venice because of the many bridges, rivers, canals, and mangroves that carve up the city. We walked through those crowded streets and prayed for the people God wanted to claim for himself.

With each passing day I was getting more excited about the possibility that we could come join the Gioppos. We would let them take the lead while we served in a support role. But while I was responding to the idea of living in this tropical city, Carol, born and raised in Minnesota, was slowly wilting under the round-the-clock heat and humidity.

As we had done in Buenos Aires, after winding up our visit with Evilásio and Mari, we checked into a hotel on the four-and-a-half-mile-long Boa Viagem Beach. Our room faced the ocean, and that first night as we went to sleep, we left the curtains drawn and the doors open to the balcony, enjoying the sound of the surf. At about three in the morning I awoke with a start to our room illuminated with a strange orange glow. It took a minute or two to realize that it was just the sun coming up over the horizon. With nothing but miles of ocean to the east, there were no obstacles, not even the heavy curtains of our hotel room, to block it. The next night we made sure those curtains were tightly drawn before drifting off to sleep.

For the next two days we strolled the crowded streets and shops near the hotel, wandered along the beach, sipped chilled coconut water, and hired a fisherman to take us for a ride across the reef on his *jangada*, a traditional fishing raft with a large sail.

But even as we enjoyed the beauty and charm of Recife, we slowly began to share with one another our doubts about the wisdom of relocating here. We had entered that phase of life often referred to as the "empty nest" with our three sons living on their own. We'd spent the previous fourteen years working with families and professionals, so the notion of reconnecting with the student culture seemed more than a bit daunting. It just didn't seem like a wise use of resources.

By the middle of 1986 we had shifted through these experiences and reviewed the related conversations multiple times. We kept coming up with the same conclusion: We had made our contribution in Brazil.

Carol came up with two very helpful analogies to describe what was happening. First, she described us as the scaffolding that goes up during construction. Once the building nears completion, the scaffolding needs to come down. Then she likened us to a family where, as the children reach maturity, it is the parents who leave home instead of the children. At the very core of an indigenous missionary effort is the concept that the missionaries work themselves out of a job. That's what we had done. It was time to move on.

But where? That was the question that was echoing in our minds.

A very significant conversation took place between me and Aldo. I remarked that perhaps it was time for us to return to the United States. His response was immediate, adamant, and precise: "You cannot think in terms of 'returning' to the USA. The Great Commission does not talk about 'returning.' It only speaks of 'going.' In the same way you left the USA to 'go' to Brazil years ago, you should now leave Brazil and 'go' to the USA."

At about that same time I received a letter from Bob Sheffield, who at that time was the director of the western division of the United States for The Navigators. He had just returned from a trip to Africa and felt God's leading to write to me.

> I don't know if you have any long-range plans or not, but I wanted to communicate with you and let you know that we would be delighted to have you in the Western Division. Future plans call for developing city ministries especially to the secularized, and I think you could really help coach us in this. Basically you could locate anywhere you would like to live and then be a part of a network of staff who have this ministry on their hearts.

That letter, along with an exchange of letters with Jim Petersen, set in motion a sequence of events. Because of the significance and long-range implications of the decision we were facing, I made a trip to the United States to meet with leadership of The Navigators in Colorado Springs. The result was a meeting that included U.S. Director Terry Taylor, Bob Sheffield, and Jim Petersen. As we started the discussion that morning, the three of them were laughing about the fact that it probably was the first time in a year they had all been in town on the same day. For me, that was one more indication that the pieces were falling into place. That meeting ended with a consensus agreement that we should be reassigned from Brazil to a city in the United States to be determined.

The next piece was a visit to Seattle and several days of meetings with local leadership of The Navigators, as well as our friends at Mercer Island Covenant Church. I flew out of Seattle a few days later with the overwhelming impression that Seattle was that city.

The Seattle flight connected at JFK with a flight to the Ezeiza International Airport in Buenos Aires, where I joined Aldo and other Navigator leaders from Latin America. This gave me the opportunity to review with these men the decision-making process to date and hear their advice and counsel. A few days later I began the last leg of my journey back to Curitiba and the final piece in the process.

Carol met my flight at the Curitiba airport, and rather than go home, we spent the next twenty-four hours in a quiet suburban hotel. That gave me time to relate in detail the conversations that had taken place in Colorado Springs and Seattle.

As we checked out of the hotel the next day and headed home, the decision was "made but not made." Whenever we faced a major decision, Carol and I had adopted a procedure that we employed once again in that circumstance. We would "make" the decision with the agreement that we would put it on hold for a stipulated period of time, anything from a few days to a few weeks. This gave us some time to "live" with the consequences and implications. If at the end of that waiting period, we were at peace, then we would "make" the decision in terms of going public with it and acting on it.

In this case, we began communicating first to our three sons, who were aware of what was happening. The hardest part was telling our friends in Brazil that we would be leaving Brazil and moving to Seattle. I wrote in a letter to a close friend in the United States, "So while the idea of 'going' is exciting, as we think and talk about 'leaving,' we choke up."

CHAPTER 28

LEAVING THE CROWD BEHIND — AGAIN

CHRISTMAS OF 1986 was a never-to-be-forgotten occasion. It was our final holiday season together as a family in Brazil. Kent had graduated from the University of Washington with a degree in computer science. He was back in Curitiba, working in a local computer service company. Dan flew in from Minneapolis, where he was well into his doctoral studies in physics at the University of Minnesota. Brian arrived from a music conservatory in Basel, Switzerland, carrying all the ingredients for our Christmas Eve cheese fondue.

The boys put in some long hours during the holidays, sorting through their books, papers, and belongings in preparation for our move. The house had been put on the market and attracted almost no buyers. Then late in December a woman showed up, walked through the house, and in five minutes made an offer. "If you leave the light fixture in the dining room and the hanging potted geraniums outside the kitchen window, I'll pay your asking price . . . and you can stay in the house until you're ready to leave the country."

The next few months went by in a blur. We negotiated with an international moving company and then had to decide what we wanted to take with us and what to leave behind. After a week of tedious sorting, Carol developed an early morning prayer: "Lord, help me to make good decisions today. And make them only once." If you've moved after living in the same place for a few years, you know the significance of Carol's prayer.

We wanted a few pieces of our Brazilian furniture to provide family continuity for the future. A cherrywood dining room set, the marble-topped coffee and end tables, and of course that big, ugly rolltop desk were going with us.

During all those years in Brazil, I had made carbon copies of most of the letters I had written to family, friends, and colleagues with The Navigators. Each year I would take that stack of correspondence and stuff it into a big manila envelope, write the date on it, and toss it into a box. Those boxes were stored on a cobwebbed shelf in our garage, and their contents provided much of the needed detail for this book.

Just ten days before our departure, I mailed off the following hand-written letter to my mother:

Curitiba, 6 April 1987

Dear Mom,

A week ago Saturday, March 28, we turned over the keys to our house. It was both a sad moment and a relief to be done. That evening there was a big buffet dinner at a hotel in our honor. Must have been over 100 people there from Curitiba, São Paulo, Campinas, Florianópolis, Porto Alegre, Joinville, and a few other places. It was quite an event. They presented Carol with a lovely gold necklace. For the two of us there was a large painting, especially painted by the artist for us, of a downtown street scene in Curitiba. It will be a special memory whenever we see it hanging in Seattle in our new home.

On Sunday there was a Domingão, a Big Sunday meeting. Instead of a message from the Bible, different ones had been asked to speak briefly about their involvement with us and with our family. Aldo summed it up as he commented that what had been accomplished was due to the grace of God, not human resources. He told about having visited in our homes and with our families in the U.S. "Ken and Carol come from simple normal families. They are like us. They did not come to Brazil with any special equipment. As God has used them, he can and will use any of us."

Following the meeting there was a big barbecue. Over 200 people. They ran out of meat after having done 187 pounds! The people from the Saturday night dinner, plus many more with a lot of children. We hardly had time to eat. Everyone wanted to talk. Then everyone wanted to say good-bye. That was the hard part.

On Thursday evening, April 16, 1987, we boarded a Varig Airlines 747 for New York City. And for the second time in our lives, we were leaving a crowd behind.

This crowd, with few exceptions, was made up of people who were first-generation followers of Jesus. They were spiritual pioneers, opening new paths into the Brazilian culture for the gospel. Their children were growing up with a God-centered worldview.

Similar to that story in Mark 5, there were people whose lives Jesus had touched and transformed and who were engaged as Jesus commanded in telling their families and friends "how much the Lord has done . . . how he has had mercy on you" (verse 19).

We could leave these very special friends behind with that same confidence expressed by the apostle Paul: "That he who began a good work in you will carry it on to completion until the day of Christ Jesus" (Philippians 1:6).

APPENDIX A

ALLELON BIBLE STUDY

THERE IS A word in the Greek language (*allelon*) used in the New Testament that when translated into English appears as "one to another." It is frequently used in the epistles to express activities and relationships among those first-century followers of Jesus. We have prepared a list of forty-eight passages where the expression "one to another" is found. When combined, they form a mosaic of life in Christ.

As you study each passage, you will observe that there are repetitions, such as "love one another." You will also see that it is possible to sort them into groups that represent similar activities or relationships. Find some friends with whom you can do this study, and then discuss your conclusions together.

Mark 9:50	Romans 14:13
	14:19
John 13:14	15:5
13:34-35	15:7
15:12	15:14
15:17	16:16
Romans 12:5	1 Corinthians 12:25
12:10	16:20
12:16	
13:8	2 Corinthians 13:12

Galatians 5:13

5:26

6:2

Ephesians 4:2

4:25

4:32

5:21

Philippians 2:3

Colossians 3:9

1 Thessalonians 3:12

4:9

4:18

5:11

2 Thessalonians 1:3

Hebrews 3:13

10:24

James 4:11

5:9

5:16

1 Peter 1:22

4:9

5:5

5:14

1 John 1:7

3:11

3:23

4:7

4:11

4:12

2 John 5

LOOKING THROUGH THE REARVIEW MIRROR: SIX CRITICAL FACTORS TO A MULTIPLYING MINISTRY

by Jim Petersen

By now it has become obvious to the reader that Ken and I didn't arrive in Brazil with a set of preconceived plans. To the contrary! All we had to go on was a single broad sense of direction that we had gleaned from our previous training and experience with The Navigators. Our goal was to raise up a generation of people who would become spiritually mature and who would, in turn, carry the gospel forward into their circles of family and friends—and eventually to other nations. Where, with whom, and how we were to do this was pretty much for us to decide.

Ken has vividly described how, in those early years, we were stripped of everything we thought we knew and knew how to do. That brought a stunning clarity to our situation. It was like walking across a beach freshly washed by a recent tide. Every footprint was our own and stood out. We could see where we had been and where our steps were taking us. We quickly saw we were headed for places we had never been before, and neither had anyone else we knew. How were we to know where to go and what to do? Where could we go for counsel?

If you've read this far, you've seen the pattern. We would find ourselves confronted with a question or an issue. We operated on the assumption that the Bible had to address that issue someplace, in some way. So we would begin to search the Scriptures for direction. Eventually, sometimes after months of searching, insight would come and we could move forward—until the next issue came along. Then the process would be repeated. We enjoyed the additional security that came with being accountable to leaders who, although they had never been where we were headed, shared our trust in the Scriptures. They would hear us out and then support us, often tentatively and with reservations. But this accountability helped us feel safe.

Now, in retrospect, as I look back on the experience as a whole, six factors stand out as being especially critical to the outcomes we saw. In the years since we lived in Brazil, I have colabored with many people working in a variety of pioneering situations around the world. I have observed that these same six factors are in play in any effort that has a vision for the long term, whether it is a church plant in Dayton, Ohio, or a gospel initiative among Muslims in Surabaya, Indonesia. I've observed that when an effort gets stuck, it is often because one or more of these factors is not functioning, but when the problem is identified and addressed, progress can resume. I include these six factors here for your consideration with the hope that they will prove useful to you as a framework for your own thinking as you reflect on your labors.

The six critical factors are:

1. Lay Foundations
2. Go to the Lost
3. . . . On to Discipleship
4. Toward Christlikeness in Community
5. Under Godly Leadership
6. Guided by a Vision for Spiritual Generations

In the following pages I will briefly explore each of these six factors.

1. LAY FOUNDATIONS

By the grace God has given me, I laid a foundation as an expert builder. . . . Each one should be careful how he builds.[1]

We were still in our first semester of language school when a classmate, a missionary who was also studying the language, invited me to drive with him to the city where, upon completion of his studies, he would begin his work as a pastor. We spent the day on the road, arriving at our destination just in time to attend a service in the church where he was planning to begin his work. We pulled up in front of a small, newly constructed church building on the edge of the town and went inside.

The service had already begun, so we sat in a couple of chairs near the back. I counted twenty-one people in the room. There was one adult male. The rest were women and children.

So, anything wrong with that?

Think about it.

A common, almost standard procedure for church planting was being followed. This fledgling church had obviously gotten its start from people investing time and money to provide the building. Then invitations had gone out in the surrounding neighborhoods, asking people to attend. That sounds normal, doesn't it?

But, as I watched, I wondered, *What message does this little group of people send to their unbelieving community about being a Christian? Would any self-respecting male who didn't already have a church background dare enter this place? How long will it take for the first leaders to emerge from within this initiative?* I worried that the next several years of my friend's life were being defined by this random approach to creating a community.

Any newly formed group quickly, inevitably gains a collective identity, an ethos. For better or worse, this ethos emits a message to the rest of the society. It sets social boundaries and determines who will and will not be comfortable participating with them. In this case, the composition of this group was reinforcing an already strong preconception in Brazil that religion was for women and children, that "real men" didn't get involved in such things.

So, how *is* one to approach a new initiative? Paul called himself an expert foundation layer. What did he mean by that? Volumes have been written on this subject, and there are certainly more to come. I don't intend to add another one here. What follows are three simple things to keep in mind as you begin your new initiative or as you do a health check on your current efforts.

1. Lay foundations on your knees.

When Jesus began his public ministry, he caused quite a stir. He healed the sick and told stories in a way no one else ever had. The crowds loved it. But he didn't let his huge public appeal get in the way of what he was really about. He would frequently leave the crowds to spend time with the few. One time, after he had gotten away from it all and spent a night in prayer to his Father, he called the few to himself and narrowed the focus of his efforts even more. He chose just twelve of them. Then he proceeded to spend great amounts of his precious time preparing them to carry his message to the world—and the generations that would follow.

Near the end of his days on earth, Jesus got alone with his Father to pray for those twelve men. He referred to them as the men "you gave me out of the world." He said, "They were yours; you gave them to me."[2]

Amazing! Even Jesus had to look to his Father for the people he had around him! We need to understand that the people we minister to are gifts from God, and our first stop as we set out to find them is in his presence. In initiating a ministry, it is far better to spend one's time praying and waiting for God to prompt and direct than it is to rush out and get something going just to feel you're doing something.

Ken told the story of how we depended on the Isaiah 45 promise as we started out our ministry in Curitiba. I don't know how you felt as you read that story, but living it was not easy. There was a desperate edge to those prayer sessions. I remember one day putting my finger on the passage and saying to God, "You're not going to waste this day too, are you?"

But I knew that the real waste of time would be for us to succumb to the temptation to invent something on our own rather than to wait for God to act. Jesus warned, "Every plant that my heavenly Father has not planted will be pulled up by the roots."[3] I realized it would be easy for us to get busy doing this and that with one group or another and then find we weren't even available when the real thing came along.

2. *Let the people you desire to reach teach you how to do it.*

The ideal is to *begin* with the kind of people you aspire to *eventually* reach. They can be your best teachers if you let them. But this isn't easy. It means seeking people out—asking them questions, listening to them, and watching their reactions. It means taking your cues from their responses and reactions. If you do this well, they will happily lead you to their friends.

The more common approach, that on the surface even seems to make more sense, is to begin with people who are already believers and count on them to connect you with others in their society. But if you begin in this fashion, you are also likely to repeat the forms and methods that have worked for you in the past. Since the people around you are already a part of the Christian subculture, they will probably accept you doing that. In fact, that's what they will expect you to do as they, too, are familiar with those same forms from their previous experiences with church.

But when you do this, you inadvertently close the door to the great majority of society that is not comfortable trying to live in your subculture. *They* would have to adapt to *you* if they wanted to receive what you have to offer.

The sobering truth is, the way you begin, the forms you employ, and the people you begin with will determine where you'll be and what you'll be doing with whom a decade later.

3. Make your foundations consist of people.

When Paul talked about the foundations he was laying, he wasn't talking about structures or organizations. He was referring to people—people he had invested his life in and whom God was transforming to resemble his Son. This meaning is made clear in his letter to the believers in the town of Colossi. He wrote, "So then, just as you received Christ Jesus as Lord, continue to live in him, rooted and built up in him, strengthened in the faith as you were taught."[4]

Peter used a similar metaphor to communicate the same idea. "As you come to him, the living Stone—rejected by men but chosen by God and precious to him—you also, like living stones, are being built into a spiritual house."[5] What's a good foundation? You have laid a good foundation when there are people who have come to love Christ and, together, live in his pursuit.

This simple idea often gets lost in our preoccupation with organizing and structuring. We commonly assume that if we can just get this thing organized and properly managed, it will go on forever. So that's where we invest our efforts. But organization is overrated as a protector of our labors. What will come of your investment will be no better than the godliness of character and the competence of the people you leave behind.

This means investing deeply in people. We obviously can't do that with everyone, but we must do it with a few. They will set the pace for the rest, and over time they will multiply. They will be there for the cruise, sustaining what has been established and taking new initiatives.

Organizations come and go. Godly people remain. If you aspire to a movement that will include future generations, investing in the few must be central to your plans as you lay the foundations.

2. GO TO THE LOST

For the Son of Man came to seek and to save what was lost.[6]

When God called out to Adam and Eve as they were hiding and asked, "Where are you?" he set the theme for the entire Bible.[7] That same question reverberates throughout the rest of Scripture. God raised up Israel so that the neighboring nations—the world—would be able to see who he is and what he's like and be attracted to him.[8] He punished disobedient Israel for the same reason—to show the nations more about who he really is.[9] When Jesus came, he simply declared, I have come "to seek and to save what was lost." Going to the lost is not an option for God's people. Indeed, we are in the world for the sake of the lost. Thus, it is a critical factor, an essential part of our calling.[10] It's what we do because that's what God is doing.

I believe the most difficult part of a new ministry initiative is to find that thread that leads to the lost and to gain those first relationships that can carry one into a network of people where rapport can be established.

When we moved to Curitiba in 1964, I had a single name to go on in the entire city. That was Osvaldo. Ken has told you his story. He has also told you how virtually all of our fruit in those early years came to us through four individuals who, like Osvaldo, introduced us to one and then another and then another of their friends.

We had to work at helping our new friends preserve their natural relational networks. Such networks are easily broken, especially when some begin coming to Christ while others are scarcely interested. We had to find ways to keep the relationships intact and continue to expand, while at the same time help those coming to faith in Christ grow to maturity. We knew that if we didn't attend to both of these needs, much would be lost.

Two ideas helped us do both: open the gospel to the interested and preserve their networks of friends.

1. Evangelism is a process.

Ken has described my first experience with Osvaldo where I made my single most important discovery about introducing people to Christ. It was the realization that evangelism is a process, not just an event. It involves planting, cultivating, and reaping.[11] I know that this now sounds like very old news, but at that time it was new news to me. It hit me as I absorbed Osvaldo's response to my "compelling" explanation of "The Bridge." When my words made no sense to him, it dawned on me that he was coming from a different starting point, one that I was unfamiliar with. Jesus described the process this way. He said, "Thus the saying 'One sows and another reaps' is true. I sent you to reap what you have not worked for. Others have done the hard work, and you have reaped the benefit of their labor."[12]

This, for me, opened up new dimensions of opportunity. It meant that although not many people are readily reapable, virtually everyone is potentially reachable. Since the seed is the "message about the kingdom"[13] and/or the "sons of the kingdom,"[14] we needed to find simple ways to sustain our sowing until the seed took root. This translated into an ongoing exploration of the Jesus story. We accomplished this through informal discussions of the Gospels, usually the gospel of John. We would do this with individuals or small groups, and we would ask just two questions: Who was that man? And what does he want of me?

Over and over again we witnessed the power of the Scriptures, even with a person who insisted he or she did not believe the Bible. I often felt like a bystander as I watched the Holy Spirit wield the Scriptures in a person's heart. There is no doubt: The Scriptures are indeed the "sword of the Spirit."[15] These regular encounters would usually continue for months before someone would conclude that Jesus had to be who he claimed to be.

The real delay always proved to be the battle with one's will. Conversion, a decision to follow Christ, is tantamount to coming out of your cave with your hands up. It is giving up your rebellion and submitting to Christ as your Lord. That's hard to do as it implies a mortal blow to one's favorite sins. We discovered that premature attempts to reap damaged the process. Where there is a pregnancy, there will be a birth. We just needed to be patient. Seldom would we be present when it occurred. But a healthy spiritual birth cannot go unnoticed. Life is obvious to all when it happens, and it's there to stay.

2. Hospitality is powerful.

Hospitality is the other form of sowing we depended upon. Once, while Jesus was at a party, he turned to his host and said,

> When you give a luncheon or dinner, do not invite your friends, your brothers or relatives, or your rich neighbors; if you do, they may invite you back and so you will be repaid. But . . . invite the poor, the crippled, the . . . blind. . . . Although they cannot repay you, you will be repaid at the resurrection of the righteous.[16]

I take this description — the poor, the crippled, the blind — as another metaphor to describe "the people in chains" Isaiah wrote about. Hospitality, bringing people into your personal home life, offers people the opportunity to get a more complete picture of who you really are and what your life is about. It's not for nothing that both Paul and Peter list hospitality as one of the requirements for leadership in the church.

You are probably wondering how we sustained the interest of nonbelievers over months while they explored the Scriptures with us and how we preserved the relational networks of their friends while this was going on. Hospitality was our answer. Hospitality provides an opportunity to be inclusive, to have the gang over, to include the skeptic and the cautiously curious. It offers the chance to let relationships grow.

But hospitality needs to be informal and fun in order for people to feel at ease. For a newcomer it is the difference between mixing with a group of friends versus walking into a strange place where you know no one and sitting in a chair, feeling conspicuous, and waiting for the program to begin. Hospitality is necessary to maintain the open texture of the group.

3. . . . ON TO DISCIPLESHIP

. . . attaining to the whole measure of the fullness of Christ.[17]

Helping people move on in their discipleship is a critical factor to any enduring ministry for obvious reasons. The alternative is chronic immaturity, which fosters perpetual dependence on the spiritual parent and also creates every other sort of problem. It is a recipe for spiritual mayhem, and there will be no second generation. Who wants to become a part of something that has *those* kinds of problems?

The Bible doesn't give us forms or formulas for helping people grow toward maturity, but it clearly states what God expects in terms of the outcomes of our work. He wants people to come to the "whole measure of the fullness of Christ." Put another way, Christ is to be "formed" in them.[18] Or they are to be "conformed to the likeness of his Son,"[19] "transformed into his likeness."[20] This is the standard God is calling his people to. But rarely, it seems, do we even come close. Why is that?

On the surface, one would think such transformation should come naturally. The apostle Paul wrote, "If anyone is in Christ, he is a new creation; the old has gone, the new has come!"[21] That should take care of it, don't you think? But is that really what happens at conversion? Yes, it is. We do go from death to life. Our identity changes to sons and daughters, to being heirs with Christ. We become citizens of the kingdom, just like that, from one moment to the next. And that's not all. We are also given the Holy Spirit to live everyday life with us. Amazing! But that isn't the whole story.

There are other things that don't change when one believes in

Christ, and that's where the battle rages. The cells in your body don't change, including your brain cells. You're still a choleric temperament, or a melancholic, with the personality to match—and you still have thirty years of bad reactions and habits that you've programmed into your character. The Bible calls all this the sinful nature. The worst of it can erupt in a nanosecond and inflict serious damage.

This brings us to the basic challenge of discipleship: What does one do with these unchanged parts? Who's responsible for what? What does God leave for the person—that only he or she can attend to? And what must one leave for the Holy Spirit—because only he can do it?

A disciple is a learner, one who learns in a certain way. A disciple learns by walking with his teacher, listening to what he says, observing what he does, and emulating his way of life. Discipleship is a form of didactics that includes apprenticeship, tutoring, mentoring, and more. It is fitting that Jesus called us to be *disciples* as knowledge really plays a secondary role in our quest for Christlikeness. Pursuing the character traits we see in him are primary. These are acquired, over time, through intimacy with the Master and dependence on the Holy Spirit. We're talking about a lifetime of growth. What's to keep a new believer on this challenging track day after day?

Having a spiritual parent makes a world of difference. It certainly beats growing up in a spiritual orphanage where you are left to try to figure things out for yourself. Paul wrote, "Even though you have ten thousand guardians in Christ, you do not have many fathers, for in Christ Jesus I became your father through the gospel."[22]

That is family talk. As the parent, Paul said, "We were gentle among you, like a mother caring for her little children. . . . For you know that we dealt with each of you as a father deals with his own children, encouraging, comforting and urging you to live lives worthy of God."[23] New believers need the individual, personal attention of a spiritual parent if they are to persevere. But they need more than that. This takes us to the next critical factor.

4. TOWARD CHRISTLIKENESS IN COMMUNITY

> From him the whole body, joined and held together by every
> supporting ligament, grows and builds itself up in love, as each
> part does its work.[24]

The popular notion that has been around for centuries—that if you're really serious about godliness, you need to withdraw from people and things and go off to live a meditative life—is just wrong. It's the other way around. If you want to grow, you need people. You need people with their needs and problems. Christlikeness can only be worked out in the course of relating to others. Think of it: Paul wrote, "Get rid of all bitterness, rage and anger. . . . Be kind and compassionate to one another, forgiving each other, just as in Christ God forgave you. Be imitators of God, therefore, as dearly loved children and live a life of love, just as Christ loved us."[25]

What part of these instructions can you follow without other people in your life? None of them. How are you going to deal with your anger if no one is around to test your patience? How will you learn to forgive if no one is there to offend you? How will you learn to love if there's no one in your life who needs anything? You need people, with their weaknesses and needs, if you are to mature. In the same way, you need others. You need to experience love, forgiveness, and grace from others if you are to really understand what God has done for you.

Interdependence

There's a second equally important reason why you need other believers in your life if you are to mature. It's that you, by yourself, aren't a complete deck of cards. God has gifted you with certain things, probably more than you can use in your lifetime. But he hasn't gifted you with everything. Instead, he has given some of what you need to others. Why? Because if you had it all, you would think you didn't need anybody or anything, and that would be to your ruin. It would be very hard for you to see the bigger picture, what you're really a part of. So that's why "God has arranged the parts in the body, every one of them, just as he wanted them to be. . . . As it is, there are many parts, but one body. . . . Now you are the body of Christ, and each one of you is a part of it."[26] This is a major truth.

The challenge for us was to find ways to *obey* these scriptures. What would a community that embodies these truths look like? Ken has told you the story of our struggles as we pursued the answers to this question. It can be done, but one has to be willing to go outside the box to do it. Achieving these biblical standards is very, very challenging, especially in our modern society where people live time-starved lives in huge, uncrossable cities. This issue needs to be at the top of our list as we deal with the questions related to the progress of the gospel in today's world. Community is, indeed, a critical factor.

5. UNDER GODLY LEADERSHIP

And the things you have heard me say in the presence of many witnesses entrust to reliable men who will also be qualified to teach others.[27]

Leader development is a critical factor to the movement of the gospel because nothing grows much beyond what its leaders are able to provide. So, Paul explained, "It was he who gave some to be apostles, some to be prophets, some to be evangelists, and some to be pastors and teachers, to prepare God's people . . . so that the body of Christ may be built up . . . and become mature."[28]

Spiritual leadership is a matter of gifted people serving others with their gifts and abilities, according to people's needs. Growing new leadership begins with understanding the things we just talked about — that the church is a body, composed of many parts, with each part making its contribution. Where this truth is in practice, the necessary leadership will be there, emerging from within. As people relate to one another, gifting becomes apparent. Everyone knows who's good at what. Some already have all they need to do their part, while others need more equipping and coaching because of the nature of their gifts.

Developing spiritual leaders must be kept in mind from the start. Ken described how we approached this; in those early "open studies" where the friends of the new believers participated, we quickly passed the leading of the discussions to the new believers. Sometimes it was awful, and the skeptics won—while Ken and I sat there biting our tongues. We knew we couldn't step in without hijacking the leader's efforts. Later, as people began feeling the need, we taught those with corresponding gifts and interest how to master the Scriptures and then teach them. We spent years coaching them in this area.

We had two goals in mind as we worked at developing leaders. First, we knew these friends would soon be scattering across the country in search of work. We wanted them to be good seed that could bear fruit wherever they "fell." Second, we were looking to make ourselves unnecessary to the movement that was being birthed. People like us shouldn't look for job security; we should look forward to being replaced. We understood that if the work we were doing was to have any permanence, it couldn't be built around us. We would need to move on. I believe, in fact, that where pioneering leaders are not thinking in these terms, they are, in effect, stunting the development of the people and the work entrusted to them. I have seen missionaries overstay in a place, and it was costly. It sends the message to the local people that they are not really needed. So they move on to other things. If your job is not open, the people you are leading will never grow into it.

Leader development follows a simple pattern. As we've observed, it begins with a person's gifts and abilities. Those gifts need opportunity for expression. They need to be acted upon. Then, when the response from others is repeatedly affirming, the person is naturally entrusted with responsibility. A commensurate authority is conceded to him by the others. "Let's have Luis do that. That's what he's good at." As this pattern is repeated, the person's responsibilities increase, as does his authority. The time will come when he will need to divide his responsibilities—and thereby reproduce himself.

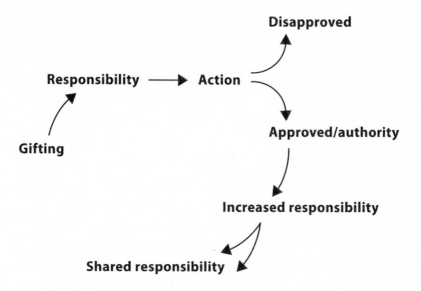

Character and Competence

Character and competence are, of course, paramount to leadership. As responsibility grows for a person, he or she must continue to develop in these two areas. Observe, in Paul's letters to Timothy, his emphasis on Timothy's continued personal development in these two areas.

As to Timothy's *character*, Paul instructed him to "fight the good fight, holding on to faith and a good conscience."[29] And then he said, "Don't let anyone look down on you because you are young, but set an example for the believers in speech, in life, in love, in faith and in purity. . . . Pursue righteousness, godliness, faith, love, endurance and gentleness."[30]

Then in addressing the matter of *competence,* Paul told Timothy,

> Do not neglect your gift. . . . Watch your life and doctrine closely. . . . Do your best to present yourself to God as one

approved, a workman who does not need to be ashamed and who correctly handles the word of truth. . . . Continue in what you have learned and have become convinced of . . . and how from infancy you have known the holy Scriptures. . . . All Scripture is God-breathed and is useful for teaching, rebuking, correcting and training . . . so that the man of God may be thoroughly equipped for every good work.[31]

Paul knew that Timothy's authority ultimately rested on the kind of man he was, not on whatever credentials or position he might have held. He was reminding Timothy of the fact that competence and godly character are lifetime pursuits. Together, they elicit trust, and trust is the basis of all true authority.

6. GUIDED BY A VISION FOR SPIRITUAL GENERATIONS

My prayer is not for them alone. I pray also for those who will believe in me through their message.[32]

Have you ever wondered why the Bible takes the time and space to record all those genealogies? It goes on for chapter after chapter, name after name; it's not exactly an exciting read.

Individuals matter, and what an individual does carries forward to the next generations. The story line of the Bible is generational. It is about God personally engaging with individuals and calling them to participate with him in what he's doing in human history—and beyond. He visited Abraham and promised him that all the nations of the world would be blessed through his offspring. Abraham's instructions were simple. He was to "direct his children and his household . . . to keep the way of the LORD by doing what is right and just."[33]

So we have the story of Abraham, Isaac, and Jacob—with Jacob's twelve sons growing into the nation of Israel—that runs through the center of the Bible. The mode for accomplishing the promise never changed. Seven hundred years after that first promise to Abraham, Moses gave similar instructions to the people: "Be careful, and watch yourselves closely so that you do not forget the things your eyes have seen or let them slip from your heart. . . . Teach them to your children and to their children after them."[34]

Notice God's intentions for Israel as the story unfolds: "I have taught you decrees and laws. . . . Observe them carefully, for this will show your wisdom and understanding to the nations, who will hear about all these decrees and say, 'Surely this great nation is a wise and understanding people.'"[35] Collectively, Israel was to be a witness to her neighbors who were watching and drawing conclusions about what this God of hers was like.[36] God was evangelizing the nations, and he was looking to Israel to carry his work forward.

This theme appears repeatedly across the Old Testament. Here is just one example: "He commanded our forefathers to teach their children, so the next generation would know them, even the children yet to be born, and they in turn would tell their children. Then they would put their trust in God."[37]

Then Jesus came along with his many stories about seeds. What a metaphor for generations! A seed contains the life of the future. For me, the most provocative use of this metaphor was the time Jesus said, "Unless a kernel of wheat falls to the ground and dies, it remains only a single seed. But if it dies, it produces many seeds."[38] He was probably talking about himself here and what he was about to go through. But then he went on to expand that meaning to include us as well. He said, "The man who loves his life will lose it, while the man who hates his life in this world will keep it for eternal life."[39]

Hate my life?! But good seed doesn't exist for itself. If there are to be generations, there will have to be death, such as giving up some of our self-absorbed pet pursuits that consume our discretionary time and resources and leave no time for others.

Jesus' prayer to his Father, recorded in John 17, is for me the final word on this subject. As he talked to his Father, he reviewed what he had done with the Twelve and his expectations for them. He said,

> I have revealed you to those whom you gave me out of the world. . . . As you sent me into the world, I have sent them into the world. . . . My prayer is not for them alone. I pray also for those who will believe in me through their message . . . so that the world may believe that you have sent me.[40]

Jesus could see the world and all the generations to come through those few men.

Sure, spiritual generations sometimes just happen, and that's always exciting to see. But Jesus was intentional about generations. We should be too, as spiritual generations are foundational to his strategy for creating his eternal family.

For us, this meant two things. First, we needed to intentionally, deliberately, and deeply invest in the people we believed God was giving us. And, second, we needed to keep things simple, reproducible.

We understood that if we were to see spiritual generations as the outcome of our labors, we needed to approach everything with that in mind. The choices we made, the methods we used, our forms—they all needed to pass the test question: When these people are out on their own, will they be able to do the equivalent?

Ken told the story of Kenneth Cooper and how he launched a movement of joggers in Brazil. He did this by writing a book on aerobics. Then, in 1970, he coached the Brazilian national soccer team in physical conditioning. When the team won the World Cup, the streets filled with joggers, mostly people who had never before run a step in their lives. All they needed to do to become a part of that movement was to don shorts and tennis shoes and hit the streets. It was that simple.

Likewise, becoming a part of the movement toward the kingdom of God is simple. All people need to do to begin is agree with a few friends to read the Scriptures and explore two questions: Who was

Jesus? And what does he want of us? Then, as they proceed together, helping each other stay on track in their pursuit of living by the truth they are discovering, the gospel spreads.

NOTES FOR APPENDIX B

1. 1 Corinthians 3:10.
2. John 17:6.
3. Matthew 15:13.
4. Colossians 2:6-7.
5. 1 Peter 2:4-5.
6. Luke 19:10.
7. Genesis 3:9.
8. See Deuteronomy 4:5-6.
9. See Ezekiel 36:20.
10. See 1 Peter 2:9-12.
11. Jim Petersen, *Living Proof* (Colorado Springs, CO: NavPress, 1988).
12. John 4:37-38.
13. Matthew 13:19.
14. Matthew 13:38.
15. Ephesians 6:17.
16. Luke 14:12-14.
17. Ephesians 4:13.
18. Galatians 4:19.
19. Romans 8:29.
20. 2 Corinthians 3:18.
21. 2 Corinthians 5:17.
22. 1 Corinthians 4:15.
23. 1 Thessalonians 2:7,11-12.
24. Ephesians 4:16.

25. Ephesians 4:31–5:2.
26. 1 Corinthians 12:18,20,27.
27. 2 Timothy 2:2.
28. Ephesians 4:11-13.
29. 1 Timothy 1:18-19.
30. 1 Timothy 4:12; 6:11.
31. 1 Timothy 4:14,16; 2 Timothy 2:15; 3:14-17.
32. John 17:20.
33. Genesis 18:19.
34. Deuteronomy 4:9.
35. Deuteronomy 4:5-6.
36. See Deuteronomy 4:5-8.
37. Psalm 78:5-7.
38. John 12:24.
39. John 12:25.
40. John 17:6,18,20-21.

ABOUT THE AUTHOR

KEN LOTTIS was born and raised in Salem, Oregon, on the banks of the Willamette River. He was the second in a family of four boys that attended Sunday school and church every week with their parents. Ken's father was a welder, machinist, and small business owner. His mother held child evangelism classes in their home. Both parents were active members of The Gideons. Even though he made an early decision to invite Christ into his life, it was not until his senior year of high school that his faith became personal. A young man in their church returned from college and took over the high school boys' Sunday school class Ken attended. That student, Roy Cooke, had been helped by The Navigators at Northwestern College in Minneapolis. He, in turn, began to pass on to Ken and the other boys in that class practical principles of living a Christ-centered life. The result was a major change of direction in Ken's life. After graduating from high school, he attended Northwestern College in Minneapolis, where he was intensely involved with The Navigators, attended Navigator conferences, and was discipled by Ed Reis for three of his four years in college. He also received training during those years from Young Life and started a club at a large urban high school in St. Paul.

Prior to his graduation from college in June of 1956 with a BA in history, Ken had made plans with Dawson Trotman to spend the summer at Glen Eyrie in Colorado Springs. With Dawson's death, that plan also died. For the next four years, Ken worked with the North America Indian Mission among the native Indians of coastal British

Columbia and southeastern Alaska. During this period, he reconnected with Carol Bauer, a classmate from Northwestern. Born and raised in Winona, Minnesota, on the banks of the Mississippi River, Carol shared Ken's small-town, blue-collar family values. They were married on October 18, 1958, in the little independent church in Winona where her electrician father had faithfully taken his family.

Early in 1960, Ken and Carol, along with their two-month-old son, left the mission in Canada and moved to Spokane, Washington, where he found a job and volunteered at a servicemen's center run by The Navigators. A year later, they responded to an invitation from the president of The Navigators, Lorne Sanny, to move to DeKalb, Illinois, and served a two-year internship on the campus of Northern Illinois University. At the end of that internship they were invited to join the staff of The Navigators, and in December of 1963, they were assigned to Brazil to team up with Jim and Marge Petersen. They arrived in Brazil on November 26, 1964, with their three small boys to begin a twenty-two-year pioneer adventure that established one of the most unique ministries in the history of The Navigators.

That boy from the Willamette and the girl from the Mississippi now live on an island in Lake Washington, where they enjoy family gatherings that include their seven grandchildren.

Interested in more titles about faith and culture?

The God Who Smokes
Timothy J. Stoner
978-1-60006-247-6

Emergent theology is raising some of the most provocative and divisive questions in the church today. Filled with humorous insights and challenging ideas, *The God Who Smokes* imagines a twenty-first-century church where hope hangs with holiness, passion sits next to purity, and compassion can relate to character.

Refractions
Makoto Fujimura
978-1-60006-301-5

Is there a world where artists and conservatives come together to create hope and healing for a hurting generation? Makoto Fujimura, award-winning artist, brings artists and conservatives, believers and non-believers, together in *Refractions*, a series of essays, thoughts, and prayers about faith and the arts.

Coffeehouse Theology
Ed Cyzewski
978-1-60006-277-3

Today's culture creates a barrier of misunderstanding in the study of God, splitting believers and keeping seekers away from a relationship with Him. Through stories and illustrations, you can build a method for theology that is rooted in a relationship with God and thrives on dialogue.

To order copies, call NavPress at 1-800-366-7788 or log on to www.navpress.com.